WINDSURFING
in a week

Peter Hart

Headway · Hodder & Stoughton

Acknowledgements

The author would like to thank the following:

Club Mistral for their excellent equipment and undying assistance and especially Ria, Phil and Christian for whom nothing was ever too much trouble.

Photographer Richard Langdon for his patience during windless times.

Phil and Ingrid Rapson of 'Flying Fish' leisure wear — the supreme hosts.

Note
Arrows ➤ denote direction of wind.

British Library Cataloguing in Publication Data
Hart, Peter
    Windsurfing in a week. – (Sports in a week).
    1. Windsurfing
    I. Title   II. Series
    797.33

    ISBN 0-340-53584-9

First published 1991

Typeset by Lasertext Ltd, Stretford, Manchester

Printed in Hong Kong for Hodder & Stoughton Educational, a division of Hodder & Stoughton Ltd, Mill Road, Dunton Green, Sevenoaks, Kent by Colorcraft Ltd.

CONTENTS

INTRODUCTION

What's it all about?

The sport of windsurfing is a mere babe in arms compared to traditional sailing. When these bizarre little craft started to appear around our coastline in the late seventies, no one could have guessed that within a decade there would be more than a quarter of a million active participants in the UK alone. At that time it was regarded by the yachting authorities as sailing's poor relation, practised by wild eccentrics who had no idea how to behave either on or off the water. As far as the average onlooker could make out, you obviously had to be supremely fit to have the slightest chance of making the thing go more than a couple of yards and would certainly spend a lot more time in rather than on the water.

Windsurfing's staggering growth and popularity reveal that such preconceptions can be misleading. Many are surprised to learn that any averagely fit person, man, woman, child or senior citizen, can learn the basics in a day. Non-swimmers and those with a chronic fear of water should channel their energies elsewhere but to the rest it offers the combined exhilaration and freedom of skiing, surfing and, in some cases, hang-gliding.

Technique, not strength, is the key to windsurfing

Many have been lured to this branch of sailing due to the uncomplicated nature of the craft which can be transported and rigged single-handed in a matter of minutes. They like the sport's accessibility; you can do it wherever wind meets water — from a lightly ruffled gravel pit to the gale-torn surf of Hawaii.

One on a board, two on a board, windsurfing is endlessly variable

On a windsurfer you are, of course, 'doing it standing up'. It is, however, the steering method which sets it apart from traditional yachts and dinghies and makes it perhaps the purest wind-powered craft. In the absence of a conventional rudder, the sailor tilts the rig forward and back to change course. Holding onto the boom, he is directly connected to the power source. It sounds very physical. Indeed, expert windsurfers are fit and strong and you too will note a pleasing change in your body shape if you persevere However, the best are like good judo players in that they economise on effort by exploiting rather than fighting the forces around them. Contrary to popular belief, learning the sport does NOT rely on well formed biceps; indeed the beefcakes who close their ears to instructions and try to muscle their way to stardom very quickly come to grief. Far more important than brute strength are the qualities of suppleness, mobility and good technique — the last of these allows you to use your bodyweight efficiently. You only have to be averagely fit to learn.

Learning — how and where

There are those who will always try to teach themselves. In the absence of any formal schools at the time, I was forced to work it out for myself ... and spent the next three years trying to shed a string of disgusting habits. In general, the DIY method is not only potentially dangerous to yourself and those sharing the same piece of water, but also desperately frustrating. You can swallow gallons to discover a point of technique which a well-informed instructor can clarify in one easy sentence. On an official course, you will be taught the sailing theory, how to rig, carry and launch the board, the simple safety code, as well as the techniques needed to sail, steer and turn round in light winds.

At a recognised RYA school, you can learn in a day on good equipment at a safe location

At a school approved by the **Royal Yachting Association**, you can be sure that the instructors are qualified and that the venue and the equipment are suitable for beginners. A full course will last for one or two days. Much of the technique will be taught on a land simulator where you are warm, dry and far more receptive to advice. On the water with your brain trying to co-ordinate a hundred and one conflicting impulses, even the simplest commands can cause confusion. Your first taste of the real thing will be on a board tethered to a buoy where you can find your balance, pull up the rig, turn round, settle in the sailing position and flounder to your heart's content without drifting away. As soon as you're through the silly stage, you will be unclipped and set free.

The RYA run a five-levels scheme which I shall tell you more about at the end of the week. You can have your progress plotted in a logbook and can be certified at every level. This logbook is internationally recognised and some centres at home and abroad need to see some proof of competence before they'll hire you a board.

About this book

There are limitations to learning from a book. It doesn't stick very well to the sail and gets soaking wet. The following pages are designed to complement rather than replace the instructor. What it can do is add flesh to the various concepts. When the course is over it can serve as a workshop manual, helping you to analyse symptoms before working out the corrective treatment and trying again.

With the week about to commence it's now time to prepare yourself for an experience which may change your life ... just remember to hold your breath!

PREPARING FOR THE WATER

Today's goals: Familiarise yourself with all the equipment — Rig and de-rig the board — Learn to recognise a good, safe sailing location

Making life easy

It looks so exciting that the overwhelming temptation is to borrow any old board and sail, head for the nearest stretch of water, throw the bits together and just give it a go — and there is no better way of making those first steps incredibly difficult and potentially dangerous. The key is to eliminate as many obstacles as possible by having the right equipment, by rigging it properly, by choosing a suitable location in a favourable wind and most importantly, by making sure you are aware of what is involved so that you can be both mentally and physically prepared.

Equipment

The windsurfer has two main components, the board itself and the rig which comprises the mast, mastfoot, boom and sail. Add to that a wetsuit, a pair of rubber shoes or boots and a buoyancy aid and you're ready to take the plunge.

At this stage of your development, it is unwise to buy your own equipment. It is better to learn on the boards and rigs provided by a school and see if you like the sport before measuring your aspirations and selecting a model that will allow you to progress.

The board

A light wind board suitable for learning will be no shorter than 3.5 m long and to offer a degree of comfort and stability to a 75 kg adult, will contain 220–230 litres of volume. Although children and lighter people do not need such a bulky board, **too big is always better than too little.**

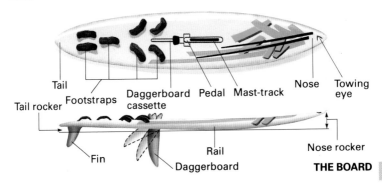

Tail   Footstraps   Daggerboard   Pedal   Mast-track   Nose   Towing eye
Tail rocker   cassette

Fin   Rail   Nose rocker   Daggerboard

THE BOARD   1

Design The board's shape is borrowed from the original Malibu surfboard. The front end (the nose) is scooped up or 'rockered' to help it ride over the waves. Its widest point and the area of maximum volume is in the middle under the mastfoot, from where the board tapers out to a narrower tail. Although it is the simplest of all sailing craft, there are a few humps, holes and protrusions which beg an explanation. Let's start at the back.

The Fin or 'skeg' as it is sometimes known, gives the board directional stability. Without it the back of the board would just wiggle from side to side like a fish's tail. In strong winds the fin has a great influence on the board's speed and turning ability.

The fin gives the board directional stability. In high winds the design exerts a huge influence on speed and manoeuvrability

The Footstraps are fitted to give the rider greater control of the board in heavy weather. **Due to their position near the back they can only be used in strong winds.** They are detachable and must be removed for learning, when they'll serve only to trip you up.

The footstraps are only needed in strong winds. For learning, unscrew them to leave a free, uncluttered deck

The Daggerboard slots into the middle of the hull. It is the board's pivot point in light winds. It makes the board more stable at rest and helps it travel upwind by converting the sideways push of the sail into forward motion. On current models the daggerboard rotates and can retract fully into the hull. In light winds, however, it must always be in the straight down position.

The daggerboard rotates and can retract fully into the hull. In light winds it must be left down to give stability and sideways resistance

The Mast-track On older boards the point at which the rig made contact with the board was a simple hole in the deck. Today it is more likely to be a sliding track with a locking unit to accommodate the mastfoot. At the back of the track lies a pedal which, when depressed by your foot, allows the mastfoot to slide forward and back. It is a useful trimming device and allows the sailor, in moderate and strong winds, to balance the board perfectly on all points of sailing. In light winds when learning, you can set it in the middle and forget about it. Most systems have a way of neutralising the pedal so that you don't activate it by mistake.

The pedal operated sliding mast-track allows you to trim the board for various conditions. When learning, leave the rig in the middle and lock off the pedal

The rig

For your first attempts it is essential to have a rig which is light, responsive and certainly no bigger than 5.5 m². Let's start by examining the various components.

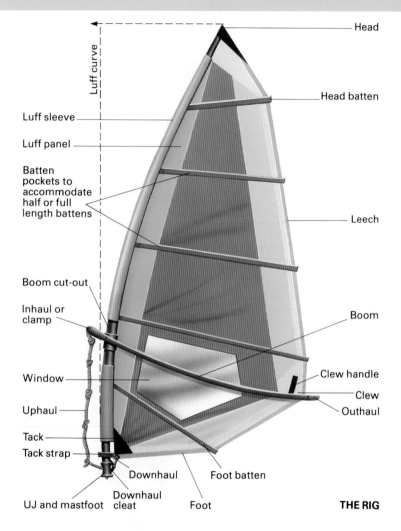

Head

Head batten

Luff curve

Luff sleeve

Luff panel

Batten pockets to accommodate half or full length battens

Leech

Boom cut-out

Inhaul or clamp

Boom

Window

Clew handle

Clew

Uphaul

Outhaul

Tack

Tack strap

Downhaul

Foot batten

UJ and mastfoot

Downhaul cleat

Foot

THE RIG

The Sail The sail is made from strong, woven polyester yarns often backed onto a clear polyester film for extra stability and stretch resistance. Battens, long strips of plastic or fibreglass, are inserted into pockets to help the sail keep its shape. On some sails they may all go right across the sail from the trailing edge to the mast; on others, those in the mid section may be half length. For learning it is wise to use the latter 'soft' option. 'Soft' in this context indicates that because the front section is unsupported, it can flap. This allows you to see how the wind is working on the sail, which in turns makes it easier to control the power in light winds.

The Mast will be about 4.65 m long. The majority of those designed for recreational sailing are made of fibreglass, which is strong, durable and inexpensive.

Masts are made of various materials but most commonly out of fibreglass. There are two-piece versions available for travelling

The Boom is the wishbone-shaped appliance you hang on to. The alloy tubing should have a soft rubberised covering to protect your palms and provide good grip. The front end will have a set of padded 'jaws' to accommodate the mast and either a rope (the **inhaul**) which loops around the mast and jams into a cleat, or the modern clamp system. The back end will have integral rollers and a cleat to help you tension the **outhaul** — the rope which attaches the bottom corner of the sail (the clew) to the end of the boom. Most booms have a telescopic back end so that they can be lengthened or shortened to fit different sail sizes.

The modern boom is collapsible with a telescopic back end to fit various sail sizes

The front end fits onto the boom with either an inhaul rope or the more modern clamp-on system

The Mastfoot/Mast extension fits into the base of the mast. Attached to it is a pulley block and **downhaul rope**, which threads through the bottom of the sail and tensions it **down** the mast. By means of a sliding collar the extension is adjustable so that like the boom it can be lengthened to fit larger sails.

The Universal Joint (UJ) is fitted to the base of the extension and is the one item which distinguishes windsurfers from all other sailing craft. Coming in the form of either a rubber joint or a mechanical knuckle joint, it allows the rig to fall in any direction. It is thanks to this 'free sail' system that the windsurfer can be steered without a conventional rudder.

Wetsuits

A wetsuit provides both warmth and protection and is essential even during the hottest summer. Wind on wet skin combined with the effort of the sport itself can produce a dramatic heat loss; the chilling effect of the wind is so strong that many semi-naked windsurfers have suffered hypothermia even in the tepid waters of Hawaii.

Wetsuits are made from neoprene rubber. There are a variety of different styles and thicknesses depending on the season, the type of windsurfing you plan to do and, of course, the colour of your eyes!

A wetsuit is essential at all times of year in the UK for both warmth and protection. They are available in different styles and thicknesses, from the one piece 'steamer' on the right with detachable arms, to the summer 'shorty' on the left

A good wetsuit will let in very little water. What water does get in should be trapped between skin and rubber where it heats up to body temperature and acts as further insulation. For the suit to be efficient it must fit like a second skin around your legs, bottom, waist and chest but be looser around the shoulders and arms to give you total freedom of movement.

The three most important qualities of a wetsuit are WARMTH, COMFORT and MANOEUVRABILITY.

Boots Although the board should have a non-slip deck, neoprene boots or shoes are vital not only to improve that grip but also to protect your feet from knocks and from sharp objects underwater in the launching area. Like the wetsuit, the boots should be very tight fitting to prevent them filling up like a pair of wellies and have a supple sole to allow subtle movement. Many expert windsurfers feel that boots cut off the electricity between board and rider and always sail bare-footed. To them, ravaged, scarred soles are an occupational hazard.

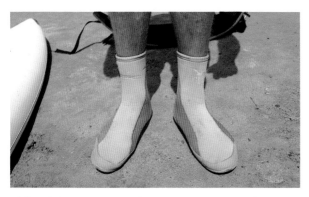

Wetsuit boots or shoes offer grip and warmth and protect your soles against the stony seabed

Buoyancy aids

If you have any doubts about your water competence, you should wear a buoyancy vest. It will make you more confident and more relaxed. In RYA centres children must wear them; they are offered to adults but are not compulsory except on waters governed by certain water authorities. It is important to note that a buoyancy aid is NOT a life jacket. That is to say, it is an aid to swimming but it will not hold your head above water should you be knocked unconscious. For the purposes of our sport the inflatable life jacket restricts movement so much that the activity is no longer enjoyable. Your wetsuit has some inherent buoyancy but in reality the best buoyancy aid is the board itself which in most circumstances is never lying more than a few feet away.

Rigging up

The attraction of windsurfing over dinghy sailing is that with only three lines to tension, the rigging up process is gloriously quick and simple. However, in order to sail effectively, your rig must be a **solid unit**. If the boom connections are sloppy and the lines insufficiently tensioned, you will have no direct control over the power source, the sail will feel like an old bag, the board will appear to have an even stronger mind of its own and worse still, there's every chance of the thing falling apart in mid-ocean. Having to sail with a hastily assembled rig is a bit like an ice skater trying to perform with skates three sizes too big.

A little extra time spent rigging can save hours of unnecessary frustration

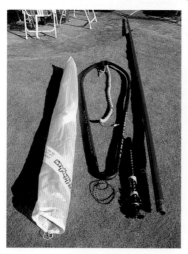

1. Lay the sail out and slide all the battens to the end of the pockets (thin end first) but do not tension them yet

2. With the battens loosened off, slide the mast up the sleeve

3. Check the base is free of grit and sand, push in the mast extension, attach the pulley hook (if there is no hook, just thread the rope through the cringle) and tension the downhaul just enough to pull the big wrinkles out of the sleeve

4. The boom must be attached at shoulder height or just below. Hold the mast upright and measure off the appropriate spot in the cut-out in the sleeve

5. Slide the boom over the sail and attach the front end to the mast. There are many inhaul systems; an instructor or dealer will explain how yours operates. Above all, the mast – boom connection must be tight

7. Now return to the downhaul. It is downhaul tension which stabilises the CE so you need to use a bit of force. Sit down, place one foot against the mastfoot and, pulling in line with the cleat, tension the rope as much as you can. There should be no horizontal wrinkles. To prevent the rope cutting into your hands, wrap it round an extension, a bit of wood or a special rig tugger!

6. Thread the outhaul rope through the rollers in the end of the boom and through the clew of the sail. Tension it and cleat it off

8. Clip the uphaul rope onto the base of the mastfoot and tie off the spare downhaul rope. With this system it can be stowed inside the mast extension

9. Tension the battens until all the creases in the pockets disappear

10. A clip-on mast pad will protect the sides of the board from the falling rig

*11. Hold the sail up on the beach and check the fullness.
The sail should fill out into a gentle curve at the front end;
too flat and it will generate no power, but if it is so full that
the cloth is touching the boom, then it will feel unstable. Having
found the perfect outhaul tension, adjust the boom so that
the clew locks right against the boom end. Similarly adjust the
mast extension so that the bottom of the sail is as near to the
deck as possible. Finally make sure that all loose ends of rope
are tied off and unable to lasso you or whip you in the face.*

Stability or lack of it, is a feature that we associate with the board *and* the rig. When full of wind, the sail has an imaginary point where all the power is concentrated. This point is referred to as the **Centre of Effort (CE)**. In a well rigged sail of good quality, the CE will remain in the same place despite a fluctuating wind, so that when a gust hits, the sail provides instant forward drive and the sailor merely has to commit more weight backwards to counteract it. In a sail which is either old and stretched, or just badly rigged, the CE wanders around as the wind gusts, forcing the sailor to move his hands up and down the boom and adopt a crude 'survival' stance if he is to have any chance of staying on board. Slick manoeuvring is out of the question.

De-rigging is the above process done exactly in reverse, that is to say, de-tension battens — release downhaul — release outhaul — undo clamp/untie inhaul rope — take off boom — slide sail off mast.

A windsurfing sail is under a lot of tension, so loosen off the out and downhaul ropes slowly to avoid shock loads which might stretch or tear the cloth.

You can leave the battens in the sail although you might have to remove the head and foot battens in order to roll the sail up. Shove them in one of the middle batten pockets to avoid losing them.

Carrying the board and rig

With good technique it is easy for the lightest person to carry their board and rig long distances. As with many techniques on the water, the skill relies on letting the wind do the work.

Carrying the board Rest it on its side and standing by the middle of the deck, grab the daggerboard with one hand and place the other in the mast-track. Keeping the back straight, lift and walk away.

With one hand in the mast-track and the other holding the daggerboard, you can lift the board effortlessly

There are two basic methods of carrying the rig, depending on whether you are walking upwind or downwind. In both cases you let the wind blow under the sail and do all the work for you.

1   **Walking into the wind** Hold the rig upright on the beach with one hand on the mast just above the boom. Grab the underside of the boom with the other hand and lift it over your head so that the mastfoot is pointing into the wind. Do not let your head rest on the window of the sail. Window material stretches and you will leave an imprint.

*To carry the rig into wind, place one hand on the mast and
one hand on the boom, and lift it over your head with the
mastfoot facing forward*

2 **Walking downwind** is effortless. With the mast lying at right angles
to the wind, grab the topside of the boom and lift the rig so that
the wind can blow under the sail; place the other hand on the mast
just to steady it.

*To carry the rig downwind just hold it out in front of you
with one hand on the boom and the other on the mast and let
the wind blow under the sail*

Simple precautions

You're nearly ready, but before leaping blindly into battle, take a little time out to consider your well being. Windsurfing has an impressive safety record and the vast majority of tricky situations which have arisen could so easily have been avoided had only the culprits exercised a little forethought and taken a few simple precautions. So to end our first day, we shall identify the potential dangers so that you can start your windsurfing career in a perfectly safe environment.

Equipment Is your equipment seaworthy? Check all the ropes as you are rigging. If they are showing any signs of wear **replace them**! No, they won't do until next time! Inspect your UJ. If there are any stress fractures, change it immediately.

The Safety Line which holds board and rig together is perhaps the most vital safety feature. If, during a fall, the mast pops out and the line is attached, the rig acts like a sea anchor and stops the board dead in its tracks; but if you forget to secure the line, the board may drift off downwind, without the rig, faster than you can swim.

Choosing a location

Inland lakes and reservoirs are most popular for learning due to the obvious safety advantages — in the event of a certain lack of directional control, for example, you will always be able to walk home. But whether on the sea or inland, the following ingredients are essential for successful learning:

Flat water Although waves will be a great source of exhilaration later on, to begin with they are only good for tipping you off.

Clear wind If the bank is covered on all sides by trees, or the bay surrounded by cliffs, then the wind will be full of holes and will tend to blow from anywhere and everywhere, making it impossible for you to settle into a comfortable stance. Select a site which offers clear access to the prevailing wind.

A safe lee shore The 'lee' shore is the one the wind is blowing to. It is where flotsam, jetsam and wayward windsurfers who cannot sail back upwind end up. On most inland waters, the lee shore is never far away. On the sea in the event of an offshore wind, it may seem like the next continent. Look to see where the wind will blow you before going out.

LOCATION

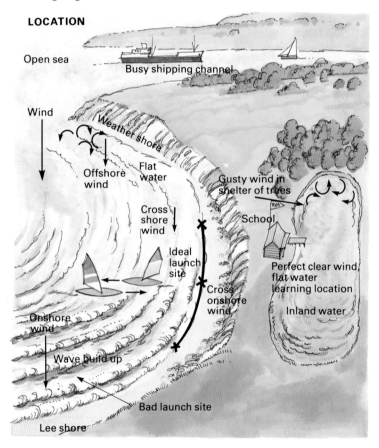

Special concerns for sea sailors

The offshore wind It is impossible to overstress the dangers of offshore winds, which are responsible for over 90% of all rescues. They are treacherous for a number of reasons:

1   The sea looks flat and particularly inviting since the wind has had no time to whip up any waves.

2   Due to obstacles near the shoreline such as buildings, beach huts, cliffs, hills, etc, the wind will be very light inshore but gets stronger and stronger as it clears those obstacles out to sea. Although just 5 mph inshore, the wind may be 30 mph 200 metres out.

3   A typical situation occurs when a windsurfer launches and heads out to sea until he finds a suitable wind. He sails happily for a while but every time he falls in he drifts a bit further downwind (out to sea) and because he is sailing with his back to the land, he is often unaware how far he has strayed from shore. Suddenly he finds himself in a wind band he cannot handle. Feeling tired he starts to sail back upwind towards the shore, forgetting that **it takes five times longer to sail against the wind than it does with the wind**. The more tired he becomes the more he falls in and the quicker he drifts from his goal. Soon he has no hope of making it back and with his rig spending most of the time in the water, he is almost invisible from the shoreline.

The message is quite simple. On the sea, DO NOT GO OUT IN AN OFFSHORE WIND!

Other water users
During your first sessions your control will not be instantaneous and left to your own devices you can be something of a hazard to other water users. Between other sailing vessels there are certain rights but avoid the problem altogether by steering clear of crowded waters. Above all, however, you must avoid commercial shipping and anyone who makes a living from the sea.

NEVER SAIL IN OR NEAR SHIPPING CHANNELS!

It's a shame to preach such a sermon of doom and gloom so early on with a big list of 'DON'Ts'. In truth, windsurfing safety is linked to the most basic common sense. Furthermore, the schools and clubs where you are likely to spend your first sessions are invariably situated at a safe location where you can sail in company and look out for each other, where there will be constant rescue cover, and where the waters will usually be free from the above mentioned hazards.

Windstrength

With the equipment properly and securely rigged at an ideal location, there is just one vital ingredient left to consider — namely the wind itself without which nothing is possible. The ideal windstrength for learning is about 4–11 mph, a force 1–3. That is a light breeze. Any less and with so little power in the sail it is very easy to get away with dreadful mistakes and so develop bad habits; furthermore the board is very slow to respond to rig movements. Any more than a force 3 and things start to happen so quickly that you'll spend a disheartening amount of time discovering a variety of dismounts.

Wind is the windsurfer's life blood. He gauges his progress by the strength he can handle, until ultimately many are only interested in near gales. Being able to judge windstrength by looking at the water surface is an essential skill not just for safety reasons, but also so you know what size sail to rig. On Friday, we shall look at the **Beaufort Scale** (wind forces 1–12), the popular means of measuring windspeed, and note how the increase of wind affects the board's performance.

TO THE WATER!

Today's goals: Launch — Pull up the rig — Manoeuvre on the spot — Set sail, turn round and come back!

Today you will experience various extremes of emotion — frustration, exhaustion and exhilaration. Within a few hours your attitude and approach will change from a frantic 'You must be joking, I'll never be able to stand on this thing,' to a more reasonable 'I really don't know what all the fuss was about' as you cruise semi-relaxed and at least partially in control towards your intended destination.

Just how quickly you make the transition from gibbering idiot back to co-ordinated human being depends on your **balance** and your **preparation** for the first steps afloat.

Balance is the one ingredient people consider essential for windsurfing. Those with good natural balance are certainly at no disadvantage but it is also wrong to think that without the aplomb of a circus acrobat you will never make the grade. Balance in windsurfing takes many forms, most of which can be taught and mastered.

Static balance is that very quality possessed by the tight-rope walker. It's the ability to remain upright on an unstable object and to some extent it is a God-given skill; nevertheless you can improve your static balance through practice. In windsurfing, static balance only really comes into play when the board is stationary and you have no power in the sail — during manoeuvres and when doing tricks, for example. Our first exercise this morning concentrates on improving static balance. Once you are moving and leaning against the sail, the rules change completely.

Arm balance Most of the time on the water it is the power in the rig which holds you up. The sail is trying to pull you one way, forcing you to lean the other and to use your body as a counter-balance. Obviously if you lean too far you will fall in backwards and if you don't lean far enough the sail will pull you forwards. This is where the arms come in, since they control how much power there is in the sail. By pushing and pulling they alter the angle at which the wind hits the sail. Very quickly these responses become automatic, and the arms constantly make fine adjustments to compensate for changes in pressure.

Dynamic balance describes the art of remaining upstanding when in motion. It is the movement of a cyclist banking in as he goes round a corner and of a waterskier or a surfer leaning into a turn to resist the centrifugal force. Dynamic balance is an essential part of strong wind sailing but will not concern you during the first part of your windsurfing career.

Preparation

The brain has trouble handling your first forays into a foreign element. The wobbly platform, the inconstant pull in the sail, the very notion of the invisible wind, all generate totally new responses which are too much for it to cope with all at once. As a result it relays a flood of 'red alert' panic impulses to the relevant body parts; hence many beginners look uncomfortable and unrelaxed. They seem to be expending an unnecessary amount of energy, their movements are jerky and they over-react to every pull and jolt. All their muscles are tense in an effort to grip the board, so they tire within minutes.

With just a bit of planning you can educate your body gradually, give it just one test at a time to concentrate on before asking it to combine the elements and tackle the real thing. Those inaugural minutes will still feel alien but 'total idiot syndrome' will be just a swiftly passing phase.

A quick splash about

Take the board out without the rig to get used to the balance. It's remarkably stable — so long as you keep your feet near the centreline

We begin the familiarisation programme by taking the board out without the rig to learn where you can and cannot put your feet. On flat water with the daggerboard down it is remarkably stable but **only if you keep your feet on or near the centreline** — the imaginary line running down the middle of the board from nose to tail. If you wander far from that line, the board will react violently to your every move, tipping you off whenever you shift your weight. As you get used to the feel, be more adventurous and wander off towards the front and back where the reduction in volume makes the board noticeably less stable. With nothing else to think about apart from balance, you can contemplate these points:

Take small steps The smaller the step and the less radical the weight transfer from foot to foot, the calmer the board remains.

Relax! When standing on dry land you don't stick your bottom out and you don't try to grip the earth with your toes so don't do it on the board! Stand up with your back straight and your weight on the balls of your feet. Relax your upper body and, keeping the feet still, maintain balance with subtle movements of the knees and ankles.

Hanging about

One of the largest barriers between many people and the ability to sail with any panache is the simple fear of committing their weight back against the pull of the rig and falling into the unknown. The fear is irrational since water is very soft should ever you collapse into it. You can overcome this fear and learn the rudiments of power control by simply holding the rig up on the beach and hanging against it — assuming, of course, there is some wind to fill the sail. We will be going into rig control in far more detail later on; for the moment, however, support the rig by the mast and place the front hand — the one which will be nearest the mast — about six inches behind the mast on the boom, and the back hand about 18 inches (shoulder width) behind the front hand. With your back to the wind and the arms straight, lean against the sail. If you overdo it just sit down on the grass/sand; if the rig feels too powerful and is pulling you forward off balance then just let go of the boom with your **back** hand — the one furthest away from the mast.

Hold the rig up on the beach and get used to leaning back to withstand the pull in the sail

Falling for fun

Now before we take the plunge, just a couple of words about this falling in lark. As long as you don't let it become an incurable addiction, falling in is an enjoyable part of the discovery process. When teaching people at all levels, I make them jump in before the session starts so that staying dry is no longer a goal. Familiar with that wet feeling and the temperature of the water, they relax, 'go for it' and improve more quickly.

As an ambitious windsurfer, you'll find a multitude of ways of leaving the board . . .

If you are nervous about the prospect of the odd involuntary dismount, you will be tense on the board and in no position at all to learn. Just remember that no harm will come to you from falling so long as you are aware of the following two situations:

If you surface under the sail don't try to claw a hole through it but just swim gently to the side — air is never more than a few feet away.

As you are falling in and as you are surfacing again, always hold a hand up to protect your head from the falling rig. You will plummet to the ocean faster than the rig (the sail can act like a parachute) meaning that the mast may be just about to hit the water as you break the surface.

Hold your breath and keep your mouth closed!

. . . but falling off is all part of the game. Just keep a hand above your head to protect it from the falling rig

Where's the wind?

And now the moment has come — action at last — time for the maiden voyage (well nearly). In this sport we can do nothing without the wind. We go because of it and manoeuvre in relation to it, **so we must ALWAYS know where it's coming from.**

To find the wind direction you can use all sorts of methods:

— Like a golfer, throw up a piece of grass. It will blow downwind.
— Flags indicate the direction; your rig itself is an ever present wind vane. If you just support it by the uphaul rope on the beach or on the water, it will flap downwind like a flag.
— Look at the water surface. The ripples blow downwind.
— Very soon you'll develop a sixth sense and will instinctively know the wind direction by the feel on your face or even the smell.

Wind terminology

When sailing there are two turns we can make; either one **towards the wind**, **upwind** or one **away from the wind, downwind**. If you think of the wind as produced by a fan, **towards the wind** means towards the source of the wind, i.e. the fan. **Away from the wind** means away from the fan.

Upwind and downwind are also referred to as **windward** and **leeward**. The windward side of the board, for example, is the side of the board the wind hits first; whilst the leeward or lee shore is the shore the wind is blowing to.

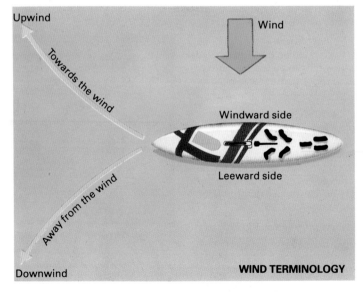

Upwind

Towards the wind

Wind

Windward side

Leeward side

Away from the wind

Downwind

WIND TERMINOLOGY

Try to avoid terminology such as left and right. They are confusing in that the direction they indicate depends on where you are facing at the time. Upwind, downwind, windward, leeward, towards the wind and away from the wind refer to the same area whatever your standpoint.

Launching

Carry the sail into the water first because the board has a tendency to float away when your back is turned, then collect the board and carry it into at least waist-deep water so you can put the daggerboard down. With the rig lying on the downwind side of the board, plug in the mastfoot, swing the board so that it's lying at 90 degrees to the wind direction and you're ready to climb on.

The first steps

Bad habits are born in the earliest stages. Getting on the board may appear quite straightforward but even in this there is a right and a wrong way. The right way is to approach from the upwind side (the opposite side to the rig), place your hands on the centreline in the middle of the board just behind the mast, heave your chest over the centreline, get onto your knees and feel for the uphaul rope. With something to hang onto, get into the crouching position, placing the front foot just in front of the mast and the back foot about eighteen inches behind, **both on the centreline**.

The wrong way is to grab the far side of the board and try to pull yourself on — you'll succeed only in tipping the board right over. The essential tip is to stay crouched, resist the temptation to stand up straight away, and **keep your feet still on that centreline**.

Uphauling

The tiresome business of having to heave the rig out of the water depresses the morale of many beginners. Even if you are learning with a very small, light rig, there are certain factors that can make the rig seem extraordinarily big and heavy:

— Water on the sail itself,
— Strong wind trying to blow it down as you pull it up,
— *Bad lifting technique*.

The water drains from the sail as soon as the mast tip is lifted clear and the wind stops trying to blow the sail back into the water once the end of the boom is free. Those first two problems disappear if you use good lifting technique.

Before tackling the specific problem of uphauling the rig, let's just look at how we should lift any heavy object. The trick lies in using the strongest muscles in your body, which are those in your legs. Take a light suitcase, place it a couple of feet in front of you, then reach forward and try to pick it up. You have to bend at the waist forcing you to resort to the toes, fingers and base of spine to do the lifting — all pathetically weak muscle groups. Now stand next to the case, keep the back straight, bend the legs, grab the case with one hand and straighten them again. It appears to be weightless.

Now transfer that technique to pulling up the rig. Still crouching, holding onto the uphaul, lean all your bodyweight against the rig on extended arms, then stand up keeping the back straight. This movement lifts the sail into the **draining position**; the hard bit is over and water now flows off the sail and out of the luff sleeve. The rig suddenly feels a lot lighter. Now just work your hands up to the top of the rope until the end of the boom clears the water and take hold of the mast with both hands just below the boom. You are now in the **secure position**.

Getting on. Approach the middle of the board from the opposite side to the rig and place your hands on the centreline

Rock forward so that your shoulders and chest are over the middle of the board

Get onto your knees and immediately reach for the uphaul rope with the front hand (the one nearest the front of the board)

With the feet either side of the mast shoulder width apart, crouch right down and lean against the rig

Keeping the back and arms straight, extend the legs so the rig is partially raised. Linger for a few seconds in the 'draining position' and let the water flow off the sail

Now the rig is lighter, work your way up the rope and grab the mast with both hands just below the boom

The secure position — arms extended, back straight, bottom in, knees and ankles slightly flexed and the rig at right angles to the board

Problems during the uphauling phase occur traditionally when you stand up too soon and lean forward, breaking at the waist. As well as risking your discs, you now have to rely on the relatively weak arms to do the work.

WRONG! Classically awful lifting technique. By bending at the waist, he can only use his arms to lift and places an unhealthy strain on his back

If you try to jerk the rig out of the water, the chances are you'll topple in backwards as it flies clear. Anticipate the drop in pull by working your hands slowly up the rope and by bringing your weight inboard as it clears the water.

The upwind recovery

In a perfect world, the rig would always end up on the downwind side with the board lying perfectly across the wind. Sadly we can't plan our falls and ultimately you will have to pull the rig up from all angles. When the rig lands on the upwind side, you will have to perform an **upwind recovery**. Climb on the board from the opposite side to the rig as before, only this time you will be facing the wind. The obvious problem is that when you lift the rig the wind will catch it and blow it straight over on top of you. In anticipation of this, lift the rig partially angling it to either the front or the back of the board; the wind then catches one side of the sail and so long as part of the sail remains still submerged, it will automatically turn the board right round until you are once again standing with your back to the wind with the rig blowing downwind. You then just work your way up the rope again and return to the secure position.

The upwind recovery. If the rig is lying on the windward side, get on the board from the opposite side of the rig as before, only this time you are facing the wind. Then lift the rig a little way out of the water, angling it either forward or back

The wind catches the sail and with the end of the boom still in contact with the water, it blows the board around . . .

. . . until you are once again standing with your back to the wind

Then just raise the rig completely and assume the secure position

The secure position

This is like a haven to which we return whenever things are not going quite according to plan. People are so keen to get sailing that they snatch at the boom as soon as they have raised the rig and so depart ungracefully. In the secure position you can catch your breath, rediscover your equilibrium, re-orientate yourself and check the wind direction — the sail always flaps downwind — before choosing a goal point and sailing away. Run this quick check down your body; the head is up, the arms are extended, the hands are holding the mast below the boom. the back is straight, the hips are forward, the knees and ankles are relaxed and slightly flexed and your weight is on the balls of your feet which are shoulder width apart on the centreline either side of the mast.

Turning on the spot

It's only natural that you should learn how to turn the board before setting sail. We do this in the secure position keeping one or both hands on the mast. The turning motion is induced just by leaning the rig against the wind either towards the front or the back of the board. **If you lean the rig back, the front of the board turns towards the wind. If you lean the rig forwards the front of the board turns away from the wind.** It is by moving the rig like this that we line the board up across the wind in the secure position before setting sail.

Using the same rig motion, we can turn the board right through 180 degrees to face the opposite direction. Naturally you will have to take up a new position on the other side of the board. Start by leaning the rig towards the back of the board. As the front turns up into the wind, take small steps around the mast, keeping your feet away from the edges. Keep shuffling around until the feet are in the same positions on the other side, at the same time leaning the rig against the wind until the board has turned all the way round and you are in your new secure position facing the other way.

Turning through 180 degrees. With one hand on the mast and using the other for balance . . .

... lean the rig towards the back of the board. As the board turns under the sail into wind, start to take small steps around the front of the mast

Shuffle the feet around onto the centreline on the new side as quickly as possible

Keep leaning the rig against the wind to make the board turn under the sail and face the opposite direction, at right angles to the wind

Note: all the way through the manoeuvre, the rig remains in the same position pointing downwind and the board just turns under the sail.

Practise this a few times to improve your mobility, turning the board round both ways through 360 degrees and then line it up in the direction you want to set off.

The sailing position

If you obey the following instructions to the letter you will get going at your first attempt. If you lunge at the rig and try to muscle it into life, it will fight back just as hard and inevitably win. So take your time and make all the movements relaxed and smooth. Discomfort, throbbing muscles and gritted teeth are signs of wayward technique.

From the secure position choose a goal point directly across the wind (a tree on the bank, a marker buoy, etc.) and make sure the board is always pointing towards it. The photo sequence reveals the correct starting technique but there are some points that must be stressed.

The balance point Your back hand is like the final connection on the circuit; as soon as it touches the boom and pulls in, the sail fills and comes alive. To withstand the force you must be in a position to lean your body away from the rig which means pulling the mast into an upright position so you can then hang off the boom like a bar. If you try to pull in too soon when your weight is forward and the mast is inclined downwind, you will immediately be pulled onto your toes, you will bend at the waist, stick your bottom out and assume the inefficient, unattractive and ultimately excruciating toilet position before dropping the rig altogether. That is why it is essential to pull the rig across the body until it can balance itself before bringing on the power. Standing upright, you should pull the rig across your body until you can see the front of the board through the window in the sail.

Sheeting in is the popular nautical term which describes the action of pulling the boom towards you with the back hand to fill the sail.

Sheeting out, not surprisingly, describes the action of pushing away with the back hand to spill wind. Look upon the rig as a door. The front hand is the hinge which stays still whilst the back hand either closes the door to capture the wind or opens it to let it out.

Setting sail. Make sure the board is lying at 90 degrees to the wind, then look along it and establish a goal point

With the front hand on the mast just below the boom, pull the rig across you to windward until it balances itself and you can see the front of the board through the window in the sail

At the same time, move the front foot alongside the mast and the back foot back slightly and turn your upper body and head to face the direction of travel. Then reach out and grab the middle of the boom with the back hand

Immediately move the front hand onto the boom so your hands are no more than shoulder width apart

Then pull the boom towards you with the back hand ('sheet in') to fill the sail and at the same time lean back gently to counteract the pull in the rig

Stance It is impossible to overstress how much your basic body posture on the board will influence your rate of progress. If you develop an efficient relaxed stance on day one, you are made for life. With a good stance, you will be comfortable, you will naturally be able to handle strong winds, you will sail fast and have good power control. If you allow yourself to slip into a cramped, stiff, hunched stance early on, you'll very quickly reach a learning plateau from which it will be impossible to budge . . . until you sort out that basic posture. Consider these points on stance:

— **Good sailors look relaxed because they give themselves room.** There is always a good distance between their upper body and the boom and it never looks as if the rig is in the way. When starting off it is easy to get tied up with the rig. As you draw the rig across to the balance point, move the feet and the upper body back BEFORE SHEETING IN.

— **Look where you're going!** In most balance sports the body is ruled by the head. In windsurfing, if you insist on looking down at your feet, not only do you risk a collision but you automatically assume a crab-like stance with everything turned into the sail. If the head looks forward over the front shoulder you can see gusts, lulls and solid objects on the water and you will naturally tend to stand up, straighten out and relax.

— **Face the direction of travel.** As you draw the rig across the body, the shoulders, hips and front foot should all turn to face the front of the board. This means when sailing your shoulders and hips will be roughly parallel to the boom and your body will be pulling directly against the centre of effort of the sail.

If comfort and style seem to be eluding you, pin the following list to your sail.

The HEAD looks forward over the front shoulder.

The SHOULDERS remain parallel to the sail.

The ARMS are extended or just slightly bent.

The HANDS grip the boom lightly and are placed shoulder width apart either side of the balance point.

The BACK is straight and parallel with the mast.

The BOTTOM is tucked in.

The KNEES and ANKLES are slightly flexed.

The FEET are shoulder width apart. The front foot is placed alongside the mast and faces the front of the board. The back foot straddles the centreline.

A good stance. The mast and body form a 'V'. The head looks forward, the arms are just slightly bent, the hips are forward and the bottom tucked in and all the joints are relaxed

Foot position. The feet should be no more than shoulder width apart. The front foot is placed either alongside the mast or just behind it, facing forwards. The back foot straddles the centreline

Turning round

This morning we turned around on the spot by leaning the rig against the wind. To turn around while on the move, you simply have to return to the secure position from the sailing position and do as before.

There are two ways to perform a 180 degree turn. You can either turn so that the front of the board passes through the wind, known as **tacking**, or so that the back of the board passes through the wind, known as **gybing**.

You'll notice when learning that it is difficult to stay upwind; this problem arises because every time you stop or fall, you drift gently downwind like all the other bits of flotsam and jetsam until you find yourself a long way below your original goal point. It helps your cause, therefore, to start by using the tack. We'll introduce the gybe tomorrow afternoon once you've learned to sail efficiently upwind.

The following technique is the simplest form of the tack. With a small sail the board will only turn in a wide arc, so start to turn well before you reach the other bank/continent and remember the following:

— When returning to the secure position always release the back hand off the boom first to depower the sail.

—You're at your most vulnerable when your feet are off the centreline. Above all do not linger in front of the mast but get the feet in their new positions as soon as possible before steering the board all the way round.

—Settle in the secure position before setting sail again. A common error is trying to grab the boom and set sail when the board is still pointing into wind. Slow down and make sure you pick a new goal point.

The basic tack. Sailing across the wind . . .

. . . release the back hand from the boom and place it on the mast

Let go with the front hand and swing the rig over the back of the board to turn it into wind

Take small steps around the mast and, holding the rig away from the body at arms length, continue to swing it around

... Get back into the secure position ...

... and set sail again

Power control

As I mentioned, by changing the angle at which the wind hits the sail you can either spill wind and decrease the pull in the sail — sheet out, or catch more wind and increase the force — sheet in. When sailing, you quickly learn to accept that the power of the wind is always changing especially on sheltered waters. Gusts and lulls force you to alter your body and rig position, or else risk falling in forwards or backwards.

The Turkish Toilet

As a beginner, the fear of falling in backwards into the unknown tends to make you lean forwards, whereupon the slightest gust can drag you into the dreaded Turkish toilet position — squatting, bottom out, back bent, rig hanging to leeward. The moment you feel your toes pushing and your backside projecting, release the power by pushing away with the back hand, stand up straight again, rock the weight back onto the balls of your feet, pull the rig back up to the balance point again and sheet in.

The back flip

If you feel yourself falling in backwards, your first reaction is to throw the rig away to leeward in the hope that it will land on the downwind side of the board in a convenient position to uphaul, and not on your head. However you can usually prevent yourself from falling in backwards in the first place, by bending the knees and throwing the hips inboard and at the same time by pulling in sharply with the back hand. This drives more air into the sail to provide the extra lift. Having sheeted in hard to save yourself, let the sail out again to its normal position. If you remain oversheeted, you will stall the sail and kill the power altogether.

Stopping

By the end of tomorrow, you should be able to steer out of trouble. There are times however, especially during your first hours, when you simply need to stop. There are a variety of ways of applying the brakes. Which method you use will depend on how dire the situation is and on who or what is in your way.

Cool and calm To come to rest gently just depower the sail by releasing the back hand. In stronger winds, however, fully battened sails will continue to generate a little forward drive even when not sheeted in.

Emergency If you need to stop on the spot, look downwind and if the coast is clear, let go of the rig completely and push it into the water. If someone is within 15 foot of you downwind (the length of the mast), then keep hold of the boom and jump in to windward.

Trick of the day

It's amazing what some people can get a windsurfer to do, **Freestyle** was born in the very early days as a means to make the light-wind days a bit more interesting and soon developed into a watery ballet with tricks being combined to form a flowing routine. Apart from being great fun, freestyle is also an excellent way of improving skills. Now on this first day, just sailing in a straight line may feel like a supreme gymnastic feat but even at this early stage we can introduce simple exercises to help improve your rig control and your own mobility and agility.

One hand and one leg Your first stunt is to sail along and try lifting one leg, preferably the front one. Then try to sail by holding the boom with only one hand. You can build up to this by moving the hands closer and closer together until they are touching and then let one hand go. The rig will feel very sensitive so be ready to react and put both hands on if things are getting away from you.

Power control. If you find yourself in the wholly undignified Turkish toilet stance, spill the power before you slip a disc ...

... by releasing the back hand. Then stand up straight, pull the rig over to windward and prepare to ease your body back to windward ...

... before sheeting in again and regaining your composure

Trying to sail with one arm and one leg is an excellent way to improve balance, board control and rig handling

Finally try to combine both tricks by sailing with just one arm and one leg. Posing is all part of being a good windsurfer!

LEARNING TO STEER

Today's goals: TECHNIQUES: Steer up and down wind — Tack upwind — Run downwind — Gybe. THEORY: The steering principle — Points of sailing

Yesterday you had some control over your destination in that you could stop and turn round. If you were heading for an object or another sailor, you could always slow down to let them pass by sheeting out, or stop by dropping the rig. Your course was limited, however, to sailing across the wind (reaching). This morning therefore, we shall look at the business of steering — changing direction up or downwind as you are sailing along.

With that mastered, we will tackle the skill of sailing upwind (beating) and straight downwind (running), finishing with the downwind turn (the gybe). By the end of today, therefore, gales notwithstanding, you will be able to sail, deliberately, to any point you wish. However, before we crawl back into those damp wetsuits (did I forget to tell you to hang them up?), here is some essential sailing and steering theory which will allow you to make sense of today's commands on the water.

Sailing theory

In the absence of a rudder, a windsurfer is steered through movement of the rig. The board has a central pivot point which is referred to as the CENTRE OF LATERAL RESISTANCE (CLR). In light winds it will lie over the daggerboard.

Correspondingly the sail has a power point near the point of maximum fullness where all the forces are concentrated. We call this the CENTRE OF EFFORT (CE).

If the Centre of Effort lies over the Centre of Lateral Resistance so that the power is acting over the middle of the board, then the board will travel in a straight line. If the rig is moved so that the CE lies either in front or behind the CLR, the board will turn and continue to turn until the rig is moved back to its original position.

If the rig is moved towards the front of the board it pushes the front of the board downwind so the board steers **away from the wind**.

If the rig is angled towards the back of the board, it pushes the back downwind so the board steers **upwind**.

To clarify this idea, place the board in the water, the rig unattached, with the daggerboard down and just try to push it sideways. If you push from the middle in line with the dagger, the whole board will drift sideways. But if you push the front, the board just pivots about the daggerboard and if you push the back, the board pivots the other way. **Your hand is acting in exactly the same way as the force of the rig.**

The difference of course is that due to the aerodynamic qualities of the sail, it also produces a forward force so that when it is upright and sheeted in correctly it drives the board in a straight line.

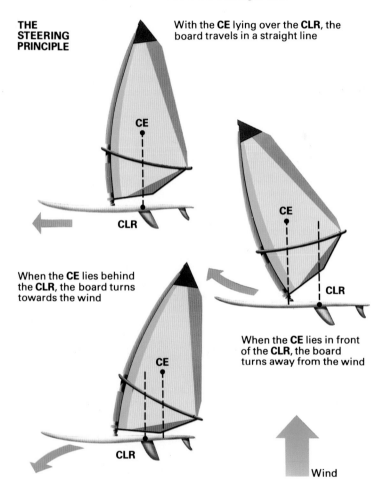

THE STEERING PRINCIPLE

With the **CE** lying over the **CLR**, the board travels in a straight line

CE

CLR

CE

CLR

When the **CE** lies behind the **CLR**, the board turns towards the wind

When the **CE** lies in front of the **CLR**, the board turns away from the wind

CE

CLR

Wind

Steering on the water

As you can now gather from the basic theory, we steer the board by tilting the rig towards either the front or the back of the board. It is very nearly as simple as it seems. However, any movement you make with the rig will result in a change in pressure and you will have to adjust your body position to compensate.

Steering upwind To steer upwind or **head up**, start from the secure position, choose a goal across the wind and set off towards it as before. When you're comfortable in your sailing position, select another goal point slightly upwind of the original one. Then tilt the rig towards the back of the board by drawing the front hand in close to the chest and by extending the back arm towards the tail of the board so that the end of the boom is almost touching the water. All the time stay sheeted in to keep the power in the sail. You will feel extra pressure in the back arm so lean against it and drive off your back foot.

Steering towards the wind. Sailing across the wind on a beam reach . . .

. . . tilt the rig towards the back of the board by pulling the front arm in to the chest and stretching out the back arm towards the tail of the board

To sail straight again, move the rig back to its upright position.
Sailing closer to the wind, the rig is sheeted in more

The board will start to turn upwind and when it is pointing towards your new goal, draw the rig back to its original sailing position. Because you are now sailing tighter to the wind you will have to pull the sail closer to the body with the back hand to keep it powered up and stop it flapping.

Steering downwind To steer downwind or **bear away** prepare as before but choose a goal downwind of your original one. Then, from your sailing position, tilt the rig towards the front of the board by stretching out your front arm and by pulling the back arm close to the chest. Even in light winds the extra force in the front of the sail is enough to pull you off balance. Anticipate, therefore, by bending the knees and keeping the weight on the back foot. Keep an eye on your new goal and when the front of the board has turned downwind and is heading straight for it, return to your normal sailing position with the rig upright. Because you are now sailing away from the wind, the sail is let out more with the back hand.

*Steering away from the wind.
Sailing across the wind ...*

*... tilt the rig forwards by stretching
the front arm out towards the
front of the board and by pulling the
back arm in tight to the chest. Resist
the pull in the front of the sail
by bending the knees and keeping
your weight on the back foot*

*To sail straight, move the rig back to its upright position and
let the back hand out now that you're sailing downwind*

Points of sailing

With your new found ability to change course, you are now mid-way through the transition from passenger to pilot. Yesterday you were happy just to be standing and went willingly wherever the board took you, but now you can more or less select your course. However, you will not be in total control of your destiny until you develop a greater understanding of your possible courses relative to the wind — your **points of sailing**.

No sailing craft can sail directly into wind. If it tries to, the sail flaps and it starts to drift backwards. The nearest it can sail is 45 degrees to the wind direction. We call the area 45 degrees either side of the wind direction the NO GO ZONE. Our aim is to keep the nautical jargon to an absolute minimum — however, there are times when the specialist terminology is neat and useful especially when describing your sailing courses. Within days the following terms will become an integral part of your vocabulary:

The beam reach is a 90 degree path across the wind — the one you followed on your first sailing session. It is the easiest point of sailing.

The broad reach is a diagonal downwind course. It is the fastest and therefore most people's favourite point of sailing.

Running involves sailing dead downwind. For reasons explained later, it is not the windsurfer's favourite.

The close reach is the course upwind of a beam reach.

Close hauled or beating describes sailing right on the edge of the No Go Zone as close to the wind as possible.

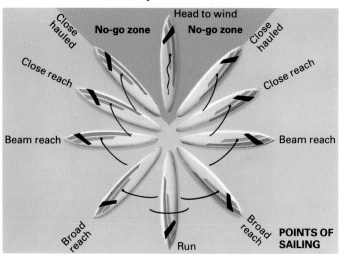

Sail trim As we have just seen, the angle you sheet the sail in to the wind will depend on your sailing course and with so much else going on, this may seem like a variable you could do without. It is however very easy to find the right angle. As you get into the sailing position, **you pull the back hand towards you just enough to stop the sail flapping and no more**. The angle between board and rig is small on a close reach with the boom pulled right in and big on a broad reach with sail let out. By varying this sheeting angle all you are doing is presenting the maximum sail area to the wind.

The sheeting angle. Note the difference in rig angle for the different sailing courses — over the centreline and close to the body for upwind sailing on the right and let out away from the body for broad reaching on the left. Note too that in both cases the upper body remains parallel to the boom

When all is not well, you may recognise these two situations:

1   **The front of the sail is flapping (luffing) and you keep turning up into wind**. You have not sheeted in enough. Leave the front hand still and forward and close the door a little more by pulling the boom towards you with the back hand.

2   **There is a lot of pull in the rig but you seem to be going nowhere**. You have oversheeted, and pulled the back hand in too far. So long as the board is not heading into wind, you can just ease the back hand away from you and the sail will once again start producing a forward force.

From the points of sailing diagram you can see there's a course and a turn we have yet to cover on the water, namely the **run** and the **gybe**. We leave them until last NOT because they are particularly difficult but because they both involve sailing downwind. Since it is all we can do to avoid making swift **involuntary** progress downwind when learning, our first priority must be to conquer upwind sailing.

Tacking upwind

Upwind sailing is like climbing a slippery slope which is so steep that you have to traverse and tread a zig-zag path to the summit. If you lose your footing and fall, you slip down a few feet. The more tired you get, the more likely you are to fall and if you keep falling you can quickly end up below your starting point.

We know when sailing that it is impossible to sail directly into wind. In order, therefore, to reach a point directly upwind, you have to sail a similar zig-zag course known as TACKING. It is not technically difficult but early on the odds seem to be against you:

Like climbing, upwind sailing is much slower than shooting off downhill/downwind. If you were to sail to a point dead downwind, it would take you roughly five times as long to get back
It is more tiring Because you are sailing against the wind and are travelling slower, there is a greater sideways force in the sail.
It can be frustrating Because the wind naturally wants to blow you downwind, you lose ground every time you fall, make a mistake or even stop for a rest.

On the positive side, upwind sailing is a great challenge; it is very satisfying and it is an excellent way to improve your skill. In competitions, the race is won and lost on the upwind legs.

The technique

There is nothing new to learn. It's just a case of combining skills already learned and above all, **concentrating**.

Choose a goal From your secure position, look behind you and select a goal on the bank or on the water directly upwind of you.

Find the edge of the No Go Zone Set sail in the normal way and then steer towards the wind by tilting the rig back. Let the board turn a few degrees before straightening up. Repeat the process until you're completely close hauled, at which point the wavelets will be striking the front of the board at about 45 degrees. If you steer into the No Go Zone so that the sail flaps and the board stops and drifts sideways then just bear away a little (tilt the rig forward) until the sail fills again; then hold that course.

Tack Sail on that course for about 200 metres and then tack using exactly the same technique you mastered on Tuesday. Adopt the secure position on the new side, set sail across the wind and then head up as

before until you find the other edge of the No Go Zone. Then keep
tacking and heading up until you zig-zag your way to your goal.

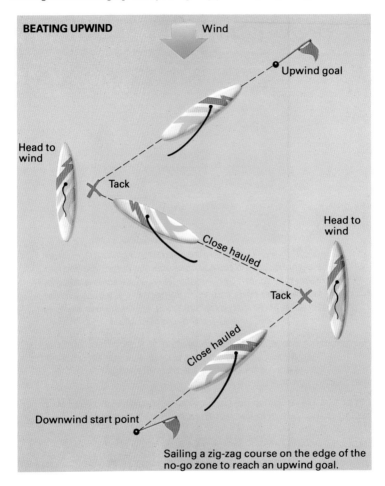

BEATING UPWIND

Wind

Upwind goal

Head to wind

Tack

Head to wind

Close hauled

Tack

Close hauled

Downwind start point

Sailing a zig-zag course on the edge of the
no-go zone to reach an upwind goal.

Problems

Without doubt most difficulties revolve around finding the tightest
upwind course. It all has to be done by feel and sensing when the
board is unhappy. Remember that the wind direction, especially on
inland waters, is not constant. You may be sailing happily on a
close-hauled course when a slight shift in the wind drops you into the
No Go Zone even though *you* yourself haven't changed direction.
Here are some solid indications that you are trying to sail too close
to the wind.

Caught in the No Go Zone. The board is too close to the wind. The sailor has pulled the sail right over the centreline and he will soon start to drift backwards. The bad stance — staring at his feet, with his body twisted into the sail — encourages him to oversheet and turn too far into wind. He must now return to the secure position and start again

The end of the boom is over the centreline If, to stop the front of the sail (the luff) flapping, you have to sheet in so far that you drag the end of the boom across the centreline, then the sail will begin to drive the board sideways and backwards.

If ever you are caught in the No Go Zone and are having trouble getting going, *return to the secure position and start again*.

Running with the wind

The next skill sounds like an athlete's gastric problem and is about as popular. Sailing straight downwind is avoided wherever possible by windsurfers, chiefly because it asks them to adopt an unstable sailing position. The rig is held at 90 degrees to the board with both feet facing the front of the board either side of the centreline. With no sideways counterbalance it is hard to cope with the unsteadying effects of waves; hence many sailors, unwisely, never learn to run and miss out on an essential skill which might be their way out of trouble in a number of situations, especially on crowded waters. In strong winds on the open sea, balancing on a run is a nightmare, and many prefer to zig-zig downwind via a series of broad reaches. On flat water, the board is wobblier that normal but not impossibly so.

Bearing away onto a run

Start as always by sailing across the wind on a beam reach. Tilt the rig right forward to steer away from the wind. Ease the boom out with the back hand to present the sail area to the wind as you turn onto a broad reach. As the board reaches the dead downwind position move both feet so they are facing the front of the board, about shoulder width apart, either side of the daggerboard. At the same time draw the rig across the body so that the sail lies at right angles to the board and you can see where you're going through the window in the sail. At this stage it helps to move both hands more into the middle of the boom.

Balance is not a problem if you heed the following:

— With the back straight keep the knees and ankles relaxed and gently flexed.
— Avoid sudden weight transfer from one foot to the other.
— Give yourself room to react by holding the rig away from you at arm's length.

Bearing away onto a run. Tilt the rig forward to bear away as before but this time let the board keep turning until it is facing dead downwind

Then stand back on the board so both feet are facing forward on either side of the centreline, a couple of feet behind the mast. Draw the rig across the body so it is square to the board and move the hands more into the middle of the boom

Steering on a run

You can alter course whilst sailing in the running position by scooping the rig to the left or the right in a sort of rowing motion. To steer left you lean the rig to the right and *vice versa*. In light winds you'll notice that the board is quite slow to react to such movements of the rig. Tomorrow, as your rig handling becomes sharper, I will show you how to speed up those changes in direction with the help of foot pressure.

Steering on a run. To turn left scoop the rig to the right ...

To turn right, scoop it to the left in a rowing motion

The gybe

The gybe is windsurfing's most illustrious manoeuvre. Twelve years on and I'm still searching for new ways to interpret and improve this incredibly diverse art which carries such unlikely prefixes as 'flare', 'carve', 'duck', 'slam', 'aerial' and 'monkey'! These are all variations of the 180 degree downwind turn.

The advantage of the gybe even in its most basic form is that you keep your speed up, unlike the tack where the board stops as it comes head to wind. In the gybe, the board appears to swoop through the turn and hence feels a lot more stable. Furthermore the foot change is simpler and there is no need to tip-toe gingerly around the front of the mast.

Gybing technique

You can gybe either from the running position or straight from a beam reach. From a run you simply release the back hand, place it on the mast, release the front hand and let the rig pivot round the front of the board. As the board turns under the sail, move the feet into their new positions on the centreline, get **secure** and sail away.

From a beam reach you lean the rig forwards as if bearing away onto a run but as the board faces downwind you just transfer your back hand to the mast, swing the rig over the front, change the feet and sail away downward without lingering.

The basic gybe. Sailing along on a beam reach . . .

. . . place the back hand on the mast and let the front hand hang free .

Swing the rig over the front of the board

As the board turns downwind under the sail, move your feet . . .

... into their new sailing positions on the centreline. As the board swings onto a beam reach ...

... you can sheet in straight away without returning to the secure position

Trick of the day

The tail sink This is a spectacular yet surprisingly easy stunt. From a run, move gradually down the board towards the back until the nose rises right up and the tail sinks. If you feel yourself toppling back, flatten the board out by leaning forward onto the boom. This is an excellent exercise to make you more sensitive to board trim and is the first step towards Thursday's flare gybe.

The tail sink. From a run, edge your way back down the board until you are standing right on the tail. If you feel yourself falling in backwards and want to flatten the board off, stretch the arms forward and lean down on the boom

THE BREEZE STIFFENS!

Today's goals: Coping with stronger winds — Getting on the plane — Learning to beachstart — Fast tacking — The flare gybe.

Today the wind has increased to a force 3, about 10 mph, what the weathermen call a 'moderate' breeze. It is the ideal strength to blow you towards the next set of techniques which involve developing your basic posture to cope with the extra forces in the sail, learning to speed up the tacks and gybes and attempting a vastly superior launching technique — the beachstart.

Sailing in strong winds

The first thing you'll notice as you launch today is that everything happens much more quickly and that the smallest mistakes are more severely punished. Above all, therefore, you'll have to adopt a positive, 'go for it' mental attitude. You cannot hope to support the rig by shivering over the centreline, but you'll have to commit all your weight against the sail, lean right out and accept a couple of dunkings as all part of the game.·

Raw aggression, however, must combine with good technique. Gritted teeth and inflated veins are not necessarily a sign that the force is being channelled in the right direction and those beefcakes who rely solely on muscle to survive will have a disastrous time next to the frail nymph who uses her weight efficiently.

Getting going

The key to strong wind expertise relies on economising on effort, on making all the movements crisp and positive and above all on **anticipating the next move. This is especially relevant when taking up your sailing position**.

You use the same basic technique learned on Tuesday but consider these slight differences:

— Due to the strong wind, you have to draw the rig further to windward with the front hand to find the balance point.
— Move your back foot further down the board (just behind the daggerboard) before you sheet in to resist the extra forward pull in the sail.
— Be especially careful to hold the rig forward with the front hand on the mast and move the upper body well back to give yourself room.
— When placing the hands on the boom, make sure they go straight into their normal positions. If you shuffle them along, you'll immediately lose control of the sail.

— Freefall! With both hands on the boom, commit your weight backwards BEFORE sheeting in and filling the sail. You can then use all your bodyweight to counteract the pull and will not be pulled forward off balance onto your toes.

— When you feel the pull, **keep the rig upright**. If you let the front hand drop away, you'll lose the rig to leeward.

Starting in stronger winds. The sailor lines the board up on a beam reach as before but this time he pulls the rig further over to windward and moves his feet further back down the board

He anticipates the pull by leaning back before sheeting right in . . .

. . . so that he is committed to windward in a position to resist the power as the sail fills

The strong wind stance

The strong wind stance. To make best use of the bodyweight, the sailor extends away from the rig on straight arms and lowers his centre of gravity by sitting down as if a chair had been placed in the water to windward. Note the head always looks forward

This next section is the most important of the week. If you develop a good strong wind stance, you will not only be comfortable, but most importantly you will sail fast and the faster you're going relative to the windspeed, the lighter the rig feels and the more you can relax and improve. It's only when you're sailing fast and **planing** (more about that later) that the more advanced funboard manoeuvres become possible.

In order to sail in the stronger winds, you do not have to change your light wind posture, you merely have to adapt it to make good use of your bodyweight.

Straight arms If you try to hang onto heavy suitcases with bent arms, your biceps and forearms will tie up in less than a minute. If you straighten the arms, the job immediately becomes a lot easier. It's the same on the board. If you sail with extended arms, you bypass the relatively weak arm muscles and transfer the load to the stronger shoulder and back muscles. Furthermore, by straightening the arms you distance yourself from the boom. This gives you two advantages: you have more room to move and react, and you can hold the rig upright and present the whole sail area to the wind even though you are leaning out. With bent arms you tend to pull the rig over your head, thereby killing much of the power.

The hands Your hands should be like hooks on the end of your arms, which just drape over the boom. Squeezing the boom and wrapping your fingers and thumbs around it in a vice-like grip is exhausting and will not make you go faster. But if your fingers are relaxed, the rest of the upper body tends to follow suit.

Sitting down In light winds, you were asked to stand up straight and tuck your bottom in. In strong winds you keep the back straight but now you sit down as if a bar stool had been placed in the water to windward. Your bottom is your centre of gravity, your ballast if you like, so by lowering it and chucking it out to windward you make yourself a much harder object to pull over.

The legs Both legs should be slightly flexed in the sitting position.

Feet The feet remain about shoulder width apart but they move further down the board. The front foot is about six inches behind the mast and the back foot is just behind the daggerboard. Like the hips, chest and shoulders, they should face the pull in the sail.

Capsizing

In winds of force 3 you may be cruising comfortably, when suddenly the board tips right up on its side. This sudden lift has been generated by the daggerboard which at a certain speed, like a hydrofoil, tries to make its way to the surface, capsizing the board in the process. Your

At a certain speed the daggerboard creates so much lift that it turns the board on its side. Either move the feet more onto the windward edge to hold it down, or roll the dagger up a few degrees to reduce the lift

first measure is to move the feet towards the windward side to hold the edge down. If the problem persists, you can reduce the lift by kicking the dagger forward a touch so some of it retracts into the hull.

Power control

If you feel overpowered in a stiff breeze, you can sheet out as normal. The problem, however, is that sheeting out disrupts your stance and throws you out of position. The board slows down and becomes less stable and with no power in the sail and no counterbalance, you are particularly vulnerable. In stronger winds, the aim is to stay sheeted in, keep the rig still and upright and compensate for minor fluctuations in the windstrength by moving the body.

It all revolves around the bottom — the ballast — which you shift in and out by bending and stretching the legs. As the wind increases, you angulate at the waist, sit down and then push your centre of gravity to windward by straightening the legs. The back is still straight and in line with the mast, and the upper body and legs form an 'L' shape. If the wind drops, you bring the weight back inboard by bending the legs and throwing your hips under the boom.

Imagine you are back on your bar stool holding the bar rail. As the wind strengthens you rock back on the stool and as it drops you rock forward. The action on the board is exactly the same.

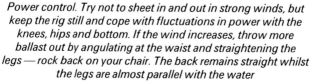

Power control. Try not to sheet in and out in strong winds, but keep the rig still and cope with fluctuations in power with the knees, hips and bottom. If the wind increases, throw more ballast out by angulating at the waist and straightening the legs — rock back on your chair. The back remains straight whilst the legs are almost parallel with the water

In a lull, bring the weight back inboard by pushing the knees and hips forward under the boom as if rocking forward on the chair

The beachstart

Now your basic rig control is automatic, there is no reason why you can't master the beachstart. It is a slicker, less tiring, safer and more efficient alternative to uphauling away from the bank/beach, where you step straight on the board and sail away without the rig ever touching the water.

We break the skill into three sections — launching the board and rig together, manoeuvring the board in the shallows, and stepping on.

Launching the board and rig together

With the board facing the water and the rig lying on the downwind side, stand upwind of them both, grab the mast with your front hand just above the boom, lift the tail of the board with your back hand, tip the board on its side, and then walk towards the water sliding it along its edge and drop it in once you're in knee-deep water.

CAUTION! The board will not perform better nor will its second-hand value increase if decorated with a row of dents and scratches; do not, therefore, take the board for a scrape across the rocks and stones and don't shove or drag it for long distances over any terrain.

Manoeuvring the board in the shallows

In order to beachstart you must master the simple technique of using the rig to line the board up in the shallows so it is lying just downwind of a beam reach.

*To launch the board and rig
together, stand on the upwind side
of the board by the water's edge.
Hold the mast over to windward
with the front hand, lift the tail with
the back hand and roll the board
onto its leeward edge. Then
looking out for rocks, push it into
the water on its nose*

*Manoeuvring in the shallows. Standing upwind of the board
in line with the tail, you can turn the board into position
just using rig pressure. Make sure the dagger is retracted and
place the front hand on the mast and the back hand on the
boom. If you push down on the boom and apply force to the
mastfoot, the nose bears away*

If you pull up on the boom, you pull the nose upwind

You never have to lift or manhandle the board into position; you stand in the same spot and use the rig to do the work.

Retract the daggerboard. With the daggerboard retracted, the board will pivot around the fin. If you apply pressure to the front of the board, you can make it swing in a circle — the fin being the centre of the circle. Standing in about knee-deep water on the upwind side of the board, hold the rig with the hands on the boom in the normal sailing position. To make the nose turn up or downwind you apply pressure up or down through the mast by lifting up or pushing down on the boom.
To bear the nose away, you push down on the boom.
To steer the nose into wind you pull up on the boom.
This exercise can be done equally well just holding onto the mast.

If you consider certain key points, the beachstart is easily achievable this afternoon:

— At all stages of the beachstart from lining up to getting on, remember your basic stance, especially your head, hand and shoulder positions.
— You control the power in the rig in two ways, by sheeting in and out as normal and also by lifting or raising the rig in the windward/leeward plane to either increase or decrease the sail area presented to the wind. It is by straightening the rig up as high as you can that you generate the power needed to pull you onto the board.
— **Let the wind pull you forward** It is tempting to try and use the boom as a bar to pull yourself up. However, if you try to heave against it, it will

give and you'll just flop in backwards. Give to the force, extend the arms and shoulders up and towards the mastfoot, stay small and compact and let the rig pull you forward onto the board like a speed boat pulling up a skier.

— Keep the back leg bent. Beachstarting is just like stepping up onto a bench. You bend the leg, rock forward and only straighten up once your centre of gravity is over your knee. The commonest fault is trying to stand up too early.

The beachstart. Line the board up so that it's pointing just downwind of a beam reach

Approach it from the rear windward quarter. Walk right into the edge and place the back foot on the centreline about two feet from the tail. Keep pushing down on the boom to stop it heading up into wind

Extend the arms and throw the rig upright to expose all the sail to the wind. Rock up over your bent back leg and swing FORWARD on your front arm. Your aim is to rise up under the boom and get FORWARD on the board

When your centre of gravity is over the centreline, bring the front leg on, staying low to resist the extra force in the sail as the board accelerates

Learning steps

Power control and board positioning are the first problem areas, so your initial task is just to take the board out into knee-deep water and practise manoeuvring it using the rig. Because your feet are on the ground, the feeling is alien but the responses should be just the same. Above all don't fight the sail. If you feel it being ripped out of your hands, just spill the power by letting go of the back hand. Use your front hand to apply pressure up and down through the rig to steer the nose. The most important tip: **always stand upwind of the board**.

Approach

'I can't get my feet anywhere near the board' is a common lament and reveals simply that the culprit is approaching the board from the mastfoot area instead of from the footstrap area. When you're ready to give it a go, push down on the rig to bear the nose away and simultaneously walk in towards the back third of the board. **Always stand just upwind of the tail, *NEVER* behind it**.

Stepping on

Check the board is just off the wind before placing the back foot on the centreline about three feet from the tail. Keep the rig low to reduce the power and sheet out when necessary. There is no hurry. You can control the board's position by pulling and pushing the tail with the back foot. To get up, stretch the arms as high as possible so you are throwing the rig up and forward. At the same time step up over your bent back knee and let the rig pull you forward. With the rig upright, pull down through the front arm to lever yourself up under the boom. The sudden straightening of the rig can produce an overpowering surge which might drag you up *and* over so be prepared to sheet out a little as you arrive in your sailing position. Put your daggerboard down again as soon as you're away from the beach.

Fast tacking

The basic tack you learned on Tuesday got you round to face whence you came. It was convenient but not much fun as you seemed to spend a long time wobbling in mid-manoeuvre. On flat water in a light breeze the balance is quite easy, but in rougher, wind-torn seas, you are vulnerable whenever your feet are off the centreline and you have no power in the sail. It is time, therefore, to speed up that basic tack, and to tighten up the turning circle. The aim is to get from one side to the other as quickly as possible. This is how it's done:

1   Rather than returning to the secure position from the beam reach, you steer the board right through the wind by tilting the rig back and sheeting in hard.
2   **Foot pressure** You are going to speed up the turn into wind by weighting the back foot and digging in the leeward rail. This sinks the tail slightly and creates a fast pivoting action.
3   **Quick steps** Once head to wind, the transition round the mast will be done by taking two quick steps, not a series of shuffles.
4   **Sheet in quickly** You transfer the mast from the old front hand to the new front hand as you step around it, dragging the rig forward and across the body before sheeting in immediately. Virtually head to wind, you then throw the rig forward to steer the board onto its new beam reach. **No matter the wind or sea state, you are secure the moment you have power back in your sail**.

Like the beachstart and many more manoeuvres to come, the fast tack calls for a touch of dynamism. The harder you attack it, the more likely you are to succeed. It's one of those strange situations where a watery grave awaits you if you try to play safe.

The fast tack. Turn up quickly into wind by drawing the rig back, by weighting the back foot and by digging in the leeward edge

Place your front hand on the mast and keep sheeting in with the back hand until the nose has passed through the wind

Then take two swift steps around the mast transferring the mast to the other hand (the new front hand)

As soon as your feet land on the centreline, throw the rig forward, sheet in to bear away and get straight into your sailing position

The flare gybe

The flare gybe is to the basic gybe what fast tacking is to the basic tack. It's a faster, tighter version which, when learned, will give you greater stability in rougher, windier conditions.

The manoeuvre has been developed from an old freestyle trick where the sailor ran to the back of the board, jumped right on the back and spun the board around on the tail in a plume of spray. The nose shot vertically into the air like a frisky stallion, hence the 'flare' prefix.

In everyday use we tone it down a bit to produce a fast downwind turn which calls on co-ordinated rig and foot pressure and a degree of mobility on the part of the pilot.

The mechanics

The flare gybe is initiated by a rig scooping action. After bearing away, the sailor sheets in and moves back down the board to within a couple of feet of the tail, his feet either side of the centreline as if running downwind. He then depresses the windward rail and scoops the rig to windward — the same movement you made when steering on a run. This creates a turning force around the daggerboard. As the board spins through the wind, the sailor moves quickly back up the board to flatten it off and kill the rotation, placing his feet in their new positions back on the centreline. At the same time he sheets out

The flare gybe. With the feet behind the mast and the knees bent, bear away by leaning the rig forward

Stay sheeted in, extend the rig away from you and move both feet back onto the tail in the running position

Depress the windward edge (the outside edge of the arc) and at the same time scoop the rig to windward

As the board spins through the wind and you arrive in the clew first position, kill the rotation by stepping forward into the new sailing position

Immediately flip the rig around by releasing the back hand, place it on the mast . . .

. . . and with little loss of speed set sail again in the familiar way

so he is sailing with the sail around the wrong way (clew first), before flipping the rig around and sailing away.

There does seem to be a lot going on. Indeed there are certain new elements which beg for explanation.

Opposite rail steering When the daggerboard is down, the board can be steered by digging in the *opposite* edge to the way you want to turn. The board only reacts, however, if you are standing right back and if you sink the tail so that the forward section of the edges are clear of the water. Only then is the board free to pivot. Naturally the deeper you sink the edge and the further back you stand, the quicker you'll spin.

The scoop In light to medium winds, you need to make a wide scoop action to initiate the turn. It helps, therefore, to move both hands more into the middle of the boom as you throw the rig to windward, remembering to move them back into their normal places before flipping the sail round.

Body angulation You spin so fast that the centrifugal force and the pull of the scooped rig are always trying to throw you off to the outside. To resist the force you must angulate at the hips like a snow skier. The upper body remains upright while the knees bend in towards the centre of the turning circle.

Killing the turn It is a common problem in the 'flare' to be surprised by the speed of the turn, fail to stop it and keep spinning straight into wind on the new side. Anticipation is the key. As soon as the back of the board has passed through the wind, start leaning forward on the rig. When it is heading on a broad reach, move the feet forward and the board will straighten up.

Clew first describes the action of sailing along with the sail the wrong way round, namely the clew pointing forward. It is the position you find yourself in as the board turns through the wind mid-way through the gybe. It is strange in so far as suddenly the roles of your hands are reversed. You still sheet in and out with the hand furthest away from the mast, although now it is effectively your front hand. In light winds you can sail clew first all day. In stronger winds, because it is the unsupported leech and not the mast which is now the leading edge, the sail feels very unstable and is likely to be tugged out of your hands. Don't linger clew first after the gybe. Once you've moved your feet, steady yourself for a second before flipping the rig. As you improve, the rig and foot change are performed simultaneously.

Flipping the rig Just like setting sail, flipping the rig around must be done with crisp, positive hand movements. From the clew first position, you always release the original back hand first (the one furthest away from the mast) to depower the sail. You then place it on the mast below the boom, release the front hand and let the rig swing round, before starting off again just as if from the secure position.

Coming ashore

Many a board has been damaged by sailors trying to sail their boards up the beach and into the car park. The idea when coming ashore is to step off BEFORE the fin hits the seabed.

Time your run back to the beach so you are sailing between waves. Retract your daggerboard, control your speed by sheeting out and approach the beach on a beam reach. When you're in about knee-deep water, step off to **windward**, then immediately grab either a rear footstrap or the tail of the board and, holding the rig to windward, shove the board up the beach (the launch in reverse).

Note: even the smallest wave can snap a mast or rip a sail, so try to keep the rig clear of the water at all times when launching and landing.

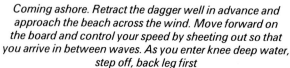

Coming ashore. Retract the dagger well in advance and approach the beach across the wind. Move forward on the board and control your speed by sheeting out so that you arrive in between waves. As you enter knee deep water, step off, back leg first

Hold the rig to windward to keep it clear of the water, grab the tail of the board and with haste, push it up the beach

Trick of the day

Sailing front to sail Here is a trick to test your power control to the limit — sailing standing on the leeward side of the board. The roles of your hands and body are reversed since you have to **push against** rather than **hang from** the sail.

It's easiest to manoeuvre into the front to sail position from a tack. Steer the board right through the wind by leaning the rig back and pulling the end of the boom right over the centreline. Then instead of stepping round the mast, just lean the rig forward and to windward so the wind fills from the other side.

With your feet still in their original positions, you control the power by sheeting in and out with the back hand, only now you pull the back hand **towards** you to sheet out, and push it **away from you** to sheet in. If you keep getting pushed in backwards, remember you can reduce the power by angling the sail down further to windward to the extent where it can balance itself and a finger's pressure is enough to support it.

69

Sailing front to sail. As if doing a tack, steer the board right through the wind, but instead of stepping round the mast ...

... ease the back hand towards and away from you to control the power

SEAMANSHIP

Today's goals: Learning to choose a good location —
Understanding tides, currents and the formation of waves — Wind
and weather — Preventing mishaps — Self rescue techniques.

Safely speaking

Windsurfing is as dangerous as the people who do it. There are
windsurfers, like mountaineers and racing drivers, for whom the
sport would be empty without an element of risk. It is the buzz they
get from sailing on the knife edge in a gale or attempting the most radical
airborne manoeuvres which keeps them going. For them the odd
bruised rib and broken nose is an occupational hazard.

But there are two categories of mishap. There are the impact injuries
described above, suffered by experts happily stretching the
performance limits. (These could only be avoided if you managed to
quell people's natural craving for adventure.) There are also
those accidents which arise out of ignorance. Sadly, windsurfing's
excellent safety record can only be attributed to the supreme
efforts of the coastguard and the RNLI. They perform literally
thousands of rescues each year, 99% of which could have been
avoided, had the victims only used a bit of forethought and common
sense.

Choosing a sailing location

Sea sailing It is wise to practise on those safe waters where you
learned, but through convenience or the desire to explore, you may take
up the challenge offered by the open ocean. The extra space, the
clearer, stronger wind and the waves can all add to the exhilaration
and the potential dangers. Unlike on inland waters where your only
concern is windstrength and perhaps air temperature, when choosing a
sea location you have to take into account the wind direction, state of
tide and many other variables. A 45 degree shift in the wind direction,
for example, can turn your idyllic riviera into a heaving cauldron of
white water.

Wind, weather and forecasts

It is a mistake we all make that like homing pigeons, we return to the
same spot time after time because we know the way, we are sure to bump
into friends or we like the pie and chips in the local cafe. From a
sailing point of view, however, it is wiser to build up a variety of
'favourite' locations which favour different wind directions.

Wind direction has perhaps the greatest influence on seastate and
sailing conditions, so let's examine the pros and cons of each.

71

In direct onshore winds, beachstarting is difficult, but if there are no waves, you can sail safely parallel to the shore. If anything goes wrong, you'll be blown straight back to the beach

Onshore winds

Direct onshore is safe in that you will be blown straight back to the beach if you get into trouble, and frustrating in that it's hard getting away from the beach in the first place. Onshore winds produce a confused messy sea, with relentless tightly spaced waves. Having to sail close hauled and tack away from the beach, you lack speed to punch through the break and can only hit the waves at 45 degrees. On flat water, onshore winds are good, allowing you to sail parallel to the beach close to the shore and often in your depth.

Cross onshore is ideal in that you will still get blown back to shore in case of emergencies, you can launch across the wind and although the waves will still be tightly spaced you can hit them on a beam reach travelling at speed. Having blown from the sea, the wind is usually constant and predictable.

Cross shore is the direction favoured by most sea sailors, particularly those who specialise in the waves. You can launch across the wind, reach straight in and out and the sea tends to be less confused. In an emergency, however, you will be blown along the beach, not straight back in. On many beaches headlands present a barrier to the sideshore wind and make it gusty.

In side shore winds you can launch across the wind and meet the waves at full speed. This is the wave sailor's favourite direction

Offshore winds

For those same reasons outlined on Monday, cross offshore and direct offshore winds are potentially lethal. Any wind blowing from the land to sea tends to be gusty and deceptively light close to shore, while the sea is temptingly flat.

As a beginner you should not even contemplate going out in an offshore wind but for ambitious windsurfers eager to meet new challenges, that advice has to be more realistic. There will be times when you'll arrive at the beach after a sixty mile drive to be met by sunshine, a golden beach and fluttering flags . . . pointing straight out to sea. Go home? Well, at some of the most famous sailing locations in the world such as Sotavento in the Canaries and Aruba in the Caribbean, the prevailing wind blows offshore. These are predominantly playgrounds for experts; nevertheless accidents still happen, but only to those whose common sense has deserted them. If you feel compelled to go out, consider the following simple but essential precautions:

— Make sure someone on the beach knows you're out there and is keeping an eye on you.
— Always sail in close company so if something does go wrong, help will be close at hand.
— Never venture more than 200 m offshore.
— Check the windstrength out to sea by asking a local or phoning the coastguard. If the wind away from the sheltered shore is very strong or due to increase, forget it!

Offshore winds are notoriously treacherous, but in controlled situations at certain locations, they can offer superb flat water sailing conditions

— Find out the water depth. On shallow shelving beaches you may be in your depth some way out to sea. In the event of a mishap you can simply walk home.

— Take frequent rests on the shore. Many tricky situations are caused by fatigue. The more tired you become, the more you fall off and the quicker you'll drift out to sea.

Tides

Tides are potentially dangerous but it is wrong to see them solely in terms of horror stories for, as we shall see, there are instances where their effect is beneficial to the windsurfer. Most importantly the coastal windsurfer must learn how the changing tide affects his or her possible sailing venue.

There are two aspects of tides you need to consider: the tide itself and the tidal flow.

The tide itself is simply a measure of the rise and fall of the water level. The extent of the tide is constantly changing. When the sun and moon pull together we get the biggest tides known as **springs**. When they are opposed the fall and rise is about half as big; these are **neap** tides. Springs occur twice a month around full and new moons, neaps occurring in between. The tides increase or decrease gradually from day to day. The state of the tide, and so the amount of water actually covering the seabed, can affect our day in many ways:

The walk to the sea! At low tide on shallow beaches, the sea disappears off towards the horizon. There's nothing wrong with a long walk, but in some instances, on parts of the UK's north west coast for example, that walk may literally be miles.

The seastate How and where waves break depends on the water depth and shape of the seabed. Wave patterns will change markedly at different states of tide.

Hidden obstructions Wrecks, rocks, sandbanks appear and disappear as the water ebbs and floods. To avoid messy confrontations when launching, landing and sailing, make sure you know where they are.

The tide's reach At some locations, the beach and launching area is completely covered at high tide as the sea floods right up to the sea wall. The obvious message is to avoid sailing around high tide.

The high tide mark To avoid the embarrassing and costly mishap of having your belongings swept away, locate the high tide mark and leave spare kit, sails, etc. well above it.

Tidal flow

This describes the horizontal movement of the sea as the water floods and ebbs. Water does not flow simply in and out but more commonly flows parallel to the shore. In many locations it is not a hazard although you will often be dragged off course when sailing back to a point on the shore. You'll quickly learn to compensate by sailing above or below your goal to allow for the water movement. In other locations the tidal stream is not so conventional. Here are some facts to note:

Flow and direction There is approximately six hours between high and low water. The tide flows fastest during the third and fourth hours, slowing down to a period of slack water. (**Note**: the tidal stream may NOT change direction exactly at high or low water.) To tell the direction of the stream, look at the revealing bow wave and wake around buoys. In light winds, moored boats lie head to tide, although in strong winds they blow round to lie head to wind.

Estuaries and channels Although the tidal stream tends to hug the contour of the coastline, it is diverted by deep water channels. In estuaries and dredged shipping lanes, the water may flow straight out to sea for some distance, producing obvious dangers for the immobilised windsurfer.

Accelerated flow Wherever a large volume of water gets squeezed or funnelled, through straits or around headlands for example, you may find tidal races flowing up to 8 knots or more.

The seastate Where the tidal flow is racing you can spot standing waves similar to those on a fast-flowing river. Where the wind blows against the tide, it's like trying to sail over a corrugated iron roof. The water surface is particularly choppy and confused with no order or pattern to the waves. On the positive side, wind against tide can produce a situation where the tide serves as an upwind conveyor belt allowing you to broad reach and gybe all day without losing any ground.

Rips and currents

Tides are not the only cause of water movement. Rip currents and undertows are produced by breaking waves and are responsible for many drownings. They are not a threat to the windsurfer, unless you are parted from your board in which case you must know how to recognise them and what to do if you are caught in one.

The undertow As a wave breaks, water is pushed up the beach and then retreats. You've probably felt it while paddling and heard it drag back the shingle. With big waves, that retreating water produces a current which can suck the swimmer back out to sea. Panic is the fatal factor, as the undertow will only drag you back as far as the next breaking wave. The trick is to relax and then try to bodysurf back in with the next wave.

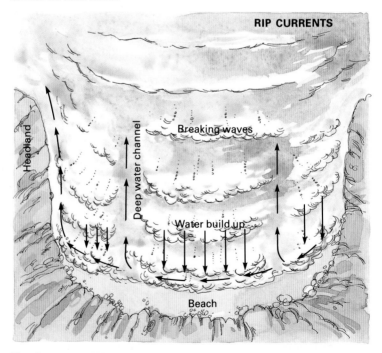

RIP CURRENTS

Headland

Deep water channel

Breaking waves

Water build up

Beach

The rip current When the surf is relentless with waves breaking one after the other, water cannot retreat back in the normal way and looks for other means of escape. As a result it travels along the beach and then finds its way back out through deep channels where the waves aren't breaking, or just follows the contour of the headland. Rips are commonly found at one or both ends of a bay. Surfers use them as a free ride back out to the break. Some rips are notoriously strong. If you do get caught in one, do NOT try to swim directly against it but swim across and out of it into still water before heading back to shore.

Waves

Waves add an extra dimension to windsurfing, one many improvers could do without. When learning new manoeuvres at any level, they are nothing but a hindrance, but ultimately they offer the short board sailor the greatest challenge and excitement. We can define waves in three categories: chop, mushy waves and swell. What you'll find will depend on the location as well as world and local weather.

Chop are the small waves you'll find inland or on the sea and are a direct result of the wind disturbing the water surface. They roll with the wind and are a reliable indicator of wind direction.

Mushy waves are ill-defined, lumpy rollers which build up and break slowly on the beach. They are also the direct result of the local wind and occur when it blows onshore or cross shore. Their size is determined by the strength of the wind and the 'fetch' — the distance between the lee and windward shores. Mushy waves tend to be tightly spaced and lack power.

Mushy waves. Onshore winds produce these ill-formed, mushy wind waves, which crumble before they have a chance to sail in a boiling cauldron

Swells arrive on beaches which face the open ocean. They form classic surfing waves — clean, powerful and well defined — rolling up the beach in sets usually of seven. They are not related to local weather but are the result of distant storms. Hence it is quite possible to have a light offshore wind blowing over a big swell. The energy from these storms travels across the ocean in lumps which then arrange themselves into long lines as they approach the beach. The more distant the storm, the longer the gap between sets.

Beautiful clean swells like this one in Australia are the product of storms often thousands of miles out to sea

Windstrength

All seafaring folk measure wind by the Beaufort Scale, which as you can see gives the wind force and its speed in knots. Rather like the fisherman's tape measure, it is also one of the most misquoted scales known to man: 'There I was screaming along in a force 8 . . .' may translate more accurately as 'hanging on for dear life in a force 4'. For your own safety it is essential to correlate wind force with water state and be familiar with the scale so you can make sense of shipping forecasts and give reliable information to others. Opposite I have taken the Beaufort Scale a step further by noting the suitability of boards, sail sizes and sailing abilities (assuming an 11–12 stone adult) next to the differing wind forces.

The Beaufort Scale of Wind Force

Beaufort No.	General Description	Sea Criteria	Windsurfer's Criteria	Limits of Velocity in Knots
1	Light air	Ripples with the appearance of scales are formed, but without foam crests.	Long boards, 5.5–6.5 sq.m. sail. Excellent for learning and light wind freestyle	1–3
2	Light breeze	Small wavelets, still short but more pronounced. Crests have glassy appearance and do not break.		4–6
3	Gentle breeze	Large wavelets. Crests begin to break. Foam of glassy appearance. Perhaps scattered white horses.	Long boards, 5.5–6.5 sq.m. sail. Upwind with dagger down, board may start to plane.	7–10
4	Moderate breeze	Small waves becoming longer, fairly frequent white horses.	Long boards, 5.5–6.5 sq.m. sail. Planing on all points of sailing. Harness use essential to avoid fatigue. Short boards now just useable.	11–16
5	Fresh breeze	Moderate waves, taking more pronounced long form. Many white horses. Chances of some spray.	Long boards, 5–6 sq.m. sail. Short, 4.5–5.5 sq.m. Perfect funboard windstrength, long and short boards plane easily at top speed.	17–21
6	Strong breeze	Large waves, white foam crests more extensive. Probably some spray.	Long boards, less than 5.5 sq.m. sail. Short, 4–4.5 sq.m. Strictly experts only. Ideal short board weather.	22–27
7	Near gale	Sea heaps up and white foam begins to be blown in streaks along the direction of the wind.	Long boards unuseable, short boards need sail less than 4 sq.m. Time for the jumping lunatics to excel!	28–33
8	Gale	Moderately high waves of greater length. Edges of crests begin to break into spindrift. Foam blown in well-marked streaks along the direction of the wind.	Short boards on tiny sails. On flat water, thin speed boards approach world record speeds (40 knots plus).	34–40

Getting a forecast

Whatever your opinion of weather forecasts, you must get one
before going sailing. The forecasts will advise you whether it's worth
putting the board on the roof at all by warning you of the extremes
of gales and flat calms. The forecast will indicate the wind direction,
whereafter you can consult the map and select a suitable beach;
and perhaps most important to your safety is that it will predict any
changes throughout the day. At certain times of year, notably spring and
autumn, weather can change very rapidly as low pressure areas track
across the country. If for example you are on a south-facing beach
and you learn that the wind is expected to swing from south westerly
to north westerly sometime during the day (as in normal in the northern
hemisphere) then you know it may turn suddenly offshore.
Forewarned, you can sail close to the beach and be prepared to
come in.

Which forecast?

Many windsurfers make meteorology their hobby. It is a fascinating
as well as useful subject, allowing them to interpret weather maps, relate
the forecast to their particular area and read the sky so they can
predict wind changes. It is a vast subject and I have suggested some
further reading. In the limited space available, however, I will just list
the sources of the best forecasts and explain some of the jargon.

Television The BBC's early and late evening news give an overall
map with windstrength and direction. The wind arrows cover a wide
area and are very general. On your local news the map is more
specific, especially in coastal areas where on occasion they even quote
the swell height. Certainly the best long term picture can be gathered
from the BBC farming forecast on Sunday lunchtime. Farmers have
an equal interest in the wind. The forecast looks ahead to the whole
week and is both detailed and accurate.

Newspapers The major dailies such as *The Times, Telegraph,
Independent* and *Guardian* all have weather maps showing pressure
readings over most of Europe and the Atlantic.

Radio On the thrice-daily shipping forecast on Radio 4 Long Wave,
the announcer works his way clockwise around the British Isles
giving up to the minute information on all sea areas. Although to the
layman it appears to be relayed in a mysterious code, the message is
easy to decipher so long as you know where the sea areas are and
which is relevant to your day's sailing. A reading such as: 'Wight . . . south
westerly 4 becoming 6 later . . . showers . . . good' reveals that the sea
area around the Isle of Wight expects winds of force 4 from the
south west strengthening to force 6 within the next 24 hours. There
may be rain showers but the visibility is good (more than 5 miles).

Gale warnings will also be broadcast at all times of day and certain everyday words have a specific meaning. 'Gale imminent', for example, means within the next six hours, 'soon' within the next 12 hours and 'later' within the next 24 hours.

Following the forecast there are the reports from coastal stations. These are particularly useful since they tell you the actual windstrength on various parts of the coast at the time of the forecast. In all these forecasts you have to read between the lines and curb your optimism for a couple of reasons:

— The sound of 'south westerly 4' may get the juices flowing in anticipation of a day at full stretch on the plane. However, the reading means 'gusting up to force 4'. The **average** windspeed may be somewhat less.
— The coastal stations themselves tend to be situated in very exposed locations with the anenometers (windspeed recorders) hoisted well aloft in clear air. The reading they give will be at least a force more than on the beach.
— The shipping forecast does not register winds of less than force 3. The announcement 'variable force 3 or less' may sound like a reasonable bet for the windsurfer but it may well mean a flat calm.

By phone *Marinecall* is a phone-in service offered by Telecom specifically for sailors. For the price of a call you phone the relevant weather station (numbers are listed in the phone book) for a recorded local forecast.

Your local seaside windsurfing shop So long as you don't abuse the service, the seaside windsurfing shop assistant is usually quite happy to look out of the window and tell you what it's blowing on the beach and what size sails people are rigging.

Self-rescue

The ability to self-rescue is essential. The knowledge that you can get yourself home and that you won't be a burden on others gives you the confidence to sail in testing conditions.

The times when you need to self-rescue arise generally through equipment failure, although there are occasions when the wind drops altogether leaving you powerless and stranded. Pages 82–3 show a quick easy method to strike for home under paddle power.

Limitations
Although few people ever do it, it is essential to practise a self-rescue every now and then. Flat water and light winds pose few problems but on a choppy sea in a stiff breeze, keeping the board on course, the rig on board and you out of the water, is an art in itself. Furthermore, trying to paddle **against** wind and waves is exhausting, frustrating and often fruitless.

Self rescue. Sit astride your board in the middle and unplug the mastfoot

Take out all the battens and store them inside the luff tube

Swing the rig round and undo first the outhaul . . .

. . . and then the inhaul or clamp before removing the boom

Roll the sail around the mast. Place the boom on the board and lay the mast on top of it with the mastfoot facing forwards before kneeling astride the mast and paddling home

If you're in trouble and need assistance, use the international distress signal. Sit on your board and cross your arms repeatedly over your head. The 'I'm OK, leave me alone, I'm just resting' sign is a clenched fist held in the air

83

Things to carry

It's contrary to the spirit of the sport to load yourself down with a rucksack bulging with life-rafts, stretchers, bone saw, etc., etc. There are, however, a few lightweight items which can fit into a harness pocket or a small bum bag, which may save the day:

A length of rope can be used for towing or being towed. It can replace broken in-, out- and downhauls and can be used to lash up a broken mastfoot or even a broken boom.

Mutli-purpose knife is needed to cut the rope. A screw driver attachment may also prove useful.

A spare UJ with the appropriate socket and nut.

A small dayglo flag for attracting attention.

Flares The small orange or red pinpoint flares are readily available and may save your life . . . but only if you know how to let them off!

So what happens if. . . ?

Emergencies arrive in the wake of the unexpected. Despite your best intentions, a sudden change in the weather, an injury or over-ambition can leave you in the unhappy situation of being incapable, or too exhausted to self-rescue. What do you do? Of course every situation is different but there are some specific guidelines which should see you safely back to shore.

If you have been becalmed, you can simply leave the rig plugged in, rest the boom on the back of the board so the rig is clear of the water, lie on the front and paddle home without having to de-rig

Sooner rather than later In strengthening winds people persevere doggedly in their attempts to sail to shore until finally they're too exhausted even to paddle home. *Recognise the danger early, stop sailing and try to self-rescue while you still have some energy.*

Never leave the board It is your life-raft. Sit or kneel on it and try to attract attention by:
— using the international distress signal
— waving your dayglo flag
— letting off a flare.

Leave the rig rigged It acts like a sea anchor slowing down your rate of drift. It is also the most visible part of your craft from the air.

Make yourself visible When sitting or lying on the board, the waves will soon completely obscure you from view. Although you can't sail, try to lift the rig into the secure position so you can be spotted from the shore.

Ditching the rig In rough seas the rig impedes your paddling progress and the temptation is to ditch it. **Only do this if you are close to shore and 100% certain of your ability to paddle home**. If you have any doubt, hang on to it for the reasons outlined above. There is always the situation where the wind suddenly abates and you'll be able to re-rig and continue sailing — but not if you've chucked it away!

Secure in the knowledge that you'll never see the inside of a lifeboat let me just sum up the day's message with the windsurfer's seven common senses.

1. **Are you and your equipment seaworthy?** Check for frayed ropes, cracked UJs, stress fractures on the mast, holes in the board and small rips in the sail. Wear the appropriate wetsuit and buoyancy and carry the appropriate spares.

2. **Let someone know where you are going and when you'll be back.** To avoid an unnecessary distress call, don't forget to let them know when you do get back.

3. **Get a local forecast.**

4. **Know your limits.** Be realistic about your sailing abilities; be cautious at first by rigging a small sail. If ever in doubt, don't go out!

5. **Sail in company.** It's a lot more fun, you push each other, learn from each other and can rescue each other. If you do see someone in trouble it's better to sail back to shore and alert the rescue boat than to create a second emergency by an act of bravado.

6. **Avoid strong tides**, offshore winds, fog and darkness. Respect the power of the sea and trouble will stay clear of you.

7. **Consider other water users.** Steer clear of busy commercial waterways and give a wide berth to anyone who makes their living from the sea. Motor should give way to sail but tell that to an oil tanker with a turning circle of seven miles!

ON THE PLANE

Today's goals: Learning to plane — Getting into the footstraps —
Footsteering — Using a harness.

Funboard sailing

Don't be confused by the bizarre terms 'funboard' and 'funboard
sailing'. The label was the product of an early 1980s marketing coup
by the Germans who were keen to make the distinction between light
wind and strong wind sailing and give a name to a new style of board.
The 'allround funboard', as it was then called, was a versatile beast with
enough volume to float adequately in light winds but which, with its
retracting dagger, footstraps and surfboard tail shape, was designed to
excel in winds of force 4 and over. Strangely the dreadful 'funboard'
tag has stuck and the word is now used to describe boards of all
lengths with footstraps and planing hulls — 99% of boards on the
market now fit into this category. But call the sport what you will —
funboarding, board sailing, sailboarding, windsurfing — it's all the
same game and it's always fun!

Far more important than quibbling over the labels is understanding
what happens to a modern board's handling characteristics in strong
winds and what the sailor needs to do to stay in charge.

*Planing. The board skims along the surface like a speed boat
with just the tail in contact with the water*

Planing If you've been for a ride in a speed boat, you will have noticed
how the boat ploughed through the water slowly to begin with
and then suddenly appeared to release and skim across the surface.

It started to **plane**. A board reacts in the same way. In winds of force 4 or more, it reaches a certain speed where it stops pushing through the water and starts to ride on top of it. You'll notice an immediate change in handling. The drag of the hull and the pull in the rig are dramatically reduced. The board accelerates and appears hardly to be in contact with the water and, try as you might, you can't prevent shrieks of sheer exhilaration flying from your mouth!

Footsteering

With the daggerboard down in light winds you steer the board by moving the rig. On Thursday, we introduced opposite rail steering — depressing the left edge to turn right, etc. — to speed up tacks and gybes. Although you used foot pressure, it was still the rig that provided the turning force with the board pivoting about the daggerboard.

If the board is on the plane and you **retract** the dagger fully into the hull to present a flat surface to the water, the board immediately changes character and starts to behave in exactly the same way as a surfboard or a waterski in that you can **bank** it into the corners so it turns along its **inside edge.** The rig provides the momentum, but it is foot pressure combined with the board's tail and rail shape which induce the turn.

When on the plane with your feet in the footstraps, you apply back foot pressure to either the windward rail to turn upwind or the leeward rail to turn downwind. The back foot pressure is crucial since most boards, long boards in particular, will only turn on the back third — the area behind the front footstraps. If the rail in front of this section grabs the water, the board will tend to straighten up and stall.

When planing with the dagger retracted, you steer by banking the board into the corner so it turns along its inside edge

It is also important to stress that the board will only footsteer if it is fully planing. The moment it drops off the plane, whether the dagger is up or down, you have to resort to conventional steering.

Retracting the daggerboard

The daggerboard, like a hydrofoil, generates lift when water passes over it. In moderate winds of about force 3 we use that lift to help the board plane early. In force 4, you can leave the daggerboard down to go upwind but on the reaches, due to the extra speed, it generates so much lift that it will actually turn the board right over on its side. Now is the time to retract it fully into the hull. To do this, head the board off the wind, sheet out and roll the top of the dagger forward with the instep of the back foot.

If you're sheeted in or are pointing upwind, you'll struggle to budge it since the lateral pressure on the dagger itself makes it stick against the side of the case.

Adjusting the mast-track

By operating the mast-track , we change the point at which the power source, the rig, makes contact with the board. By sliding the rig forward or back we increase or decrease the board's **waterline length and wetted surface** — namely how much of it stays in contact with the water. We also affect the trim — the angle at which it rides in the water. When learning to cope with strong winds, getting on the plane and using the footstraps, you can leave it in the middle and the board will still perform; but now is the time to experiment and see how the board reacts to different track positions.

If you leave the rig forward in the track when sailing upwind in a stiff breeze with the dagger down, the weight of the rig encourages the leeward rail to bite in the water and improves lateral resistance. With the CE forward, the board is better behaved in a straight line

With the track back and the dagger retracted, the board will be slower to rise onto plane but will feel more manoeuvrable with a higher top speed

Rig forward in the track:
— The board lies flat on the water so it planes earlier
— The wetted surface is increased so the reaching speed is limited
— The board is less sensitive to footsteering
— The nose tends to dig into waves
— Strong wind windward performance with the dagger down improves. The extra waterline length provides more lateral resistance and with the sail's CE forward, the board is easier to control.

Rig back in the track:
— With the weight of the sailor and the rig over the back of the board, the tail is slower to rise up onto the plane
— The wetted surface and the drag are reduced so the board has a higher top speed
— With the front section clear of the water, the board is more lively and manoeuvrable
— The board is hard to drive to windward. With the dagger down it rounds up into wind and is likely to capsize
— With the rig nearer the back of the board, it's easier to move back into the footstraps.

Operating the track is done by depressing the pedal with the front foot and then applying pressure to the boom. To move the rig back, stay sheeted in and lift up on the boom. To move the rig forward, sheet **out**, angle the mast back slightly and push down on the boom.

Distributing the forces

In light winds we stand more or less in the middle of the board and hold the rig upright. The power of the rig is transferred down into the middle of the board and with the daggerboard converting the sideways forces into forward motion, the board bumbles off in a straight line. But in planing winds, such a stance just doesn't work. The board's planing surface is the back third of the board; if we stand in the middle, we keep pushing the front section into the water and prevent the board from rising up onto that reduced area.

Every sailor at this level notes that the footstraps are mounted over the back third of the board. They correctly assume that this is where they are supposed to stand in strong winds but without exception, the same question springs to their lips: *How can you stand so far back on the board without sinking the tail and heading up into wind?*

The fulcrum effect

It is a simple case of understanding how the power from the rig makes the board go along. That power is transferred into the board via two points, your feet and the mastfoot, and how the sailor distributes that power determines the angle the board rides in the water and whether it goes straight.

Imagine that the board is a see-saw with a fulcrum in the middle. Your aim is to balance it level so neither the front nor the back touch the ground. If you stand near the back, the back will sink down unless you counteract that movement by increasing the pressure through the mastfoot. You do that simply by hanging out forward and to windward off the rig to take some of the weight off your feet.

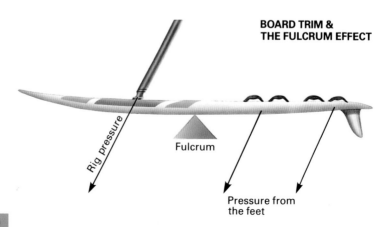

**BOARD TRIM &
THE FULCRUM EFFECT**

Rig pressure

Fulcrum

Pressure from
the feet

Your chief aim when sailing in planing conditions is to keep balancing the board despite changing winds and bumpy seas **so that it is riding flat at a constant angle**. As we shall see, the distribution of power through the feet and rig changes as the board accelerates and other forces come into play.

Footstraps

In everyday use, straps provide stability and control on all lengths of board in strong winds. When hiked out to windward your weight acts sideways against the board and the feet can easily slide off — a problem compounded by waves and water washing over the board. With your feet in the straps you are not only more secure but you are a part of the board and can use the slightest toe and heel pressure to alter the trim and keep the board riding flat at its most efficient angle.

A long board may have as many as ten footstraps: two sets of beating straps mounted near the edge for use when the dagger is down; behind them a front and rear set of reaching straps for the front foot, angled diagonally in towards the sail, and on the tail a choice of two straps for the back foot. The further back you stand the livelier and faster the

FOOTSTRAPS

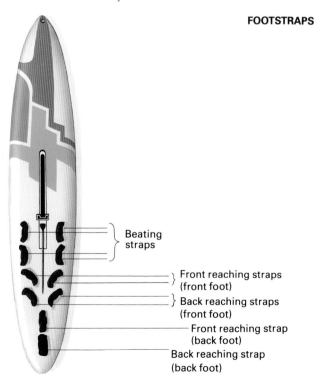

Beating straps

Front reaching straps
(front foot)

Back reaching straps
(front foot)

Front reaching strap
(back foot)

Back reaching strap
(back foot)

board will be and the harder it is to control. To begin with, aim to sail in the front set of reaching straps. Once you're familiar with the feeling of standing so far back, you can edge towards the rear set and sail the board right from the tail.

Adjusting the straps Most straps have a double velcro fastening system and are instantly adjustable. It is essential, for safety and performance reasons, that they fit correctly.

The straps should fit tightly across the widest part of your foot. In the back strap, for example, your toes should just poke through far enough to straddle the centreline.

Many boards these day come fitted with two parallel back straps. These are designed so your foot conforms to the dome of the tail and the heel can push against the side of the board.

If the straps are too loose, you will lose direct control of the board and there's a danger that after a fall, a foot could slide right through and get trapped.

If the straps are too tight, your feet will be too near the windward edge, they'll sink the rail and drag in the water causing the board to head up into wind.

Thanks to a velcro webbing system, the footstraps are easily adjustable

The strap must fit tightly across the widest part of the foot. The back foot slides in so the toes just straddle the centreline

Carrying board and rig on the downwind side is safe and easy in all windstrengths. The front hand holds the front footstrap and the back hand holds the top of the boom. Rest the board on your thighs and let wind blow under the rig

In moderate winds you can lift shorter boards by holding the front strap with the back hand and drawing the sail over your head with the front hand

Carrying the board and rig together

Now that you've fitted the footstraps it's quite possible to carry board and rig clear of the ground for quite long distances. The key as always is to let the wind blow under the equipment and do the work for you.

The universal method is to stand upwind of the board and rig. With the mast parallel to the wind, grab the top of the boom with the back hand and a front footstrap with the front hand. Lift them both up and balance the board on your upper thigh.

A popular alternative for long distances is to walk with the board and rig either side of you

With smaller boards, a popular method in moderate winds is to hold the mast with the front hand, grab the windward front footstrap with the back hand and lift so that the rig is flying above your head. BEWARE! If you rest your head on the window material, it will stretch to leave an unsightly imprint.

Getting into the footstraps

Although it's not good teaching practice to introduce negative thoughts, it's interesting to note that the novice funboarder's most common lament is that he can't get anywhere near the footstraps without the board heading up into wind. Now on a wholly positive note, the malaise is immediately curable so long as you remember that you can only get into the footstraps:
— in winds of force 4 and above,
— when the board is beginning to plane with the dagger retracted,
— if your stance is good and relaxed.

The aim as you first set off is to take the weight off your feet by hanging off the boom to allow the tail to rise up and release. At the same time hold the rig forward so its weight and power hold the nose down and keep the board level.

As the board picks up speed, like a waterski being pulled through the water, it creates its own lift. Likewise when water starts to pass over the foil of the fin, it too creates lift like a small daggerboard. To counteract this lift you shift more weight back onto the feet to hold the board in the water and stop it skipping around.
In fresh to strong winds of force 5 or more, you need to direct most of the sail's force through the feet. In marginal planing winds of force 4, you hang more weight off the rig.

Getting into the footstraps. Standing in the middle of the board with both hands on the boom ...

... move the back foot back onto the centreline between the front and back straps. Sink right down to take your weight on the rig and extend away from the boom by straightening the arms

With the back foot trimming the board flat and still forcing your weight down through the boom, wait for the board to pick up speed before lifting the front foot into the front reaching strap

Staying sheeted in, move your weight back onto your feet and place the back foot in the back strap as the board accelerates towards terminal velocity

Closing the slot. Once you have reached maximum speed and the board is planing on the minimum area, you can draw the rig back to close the gap off between the deck of the board and the foot of the sail

Closing the slot Now that the dagger is retracted, the board's CLR, its pivot point, can move back as the board rises onto the plane and less and less of it makes contact with the water. This allows you to draw the rig back without steering the board into wind. When you're at full speed, planing just on the tail, you can angle the rig so far back that you close off the gap or 'slot' between the foot of the sail and the deck of the board. This is the most efficient rig position.

Harness technique

It won't have taken you long to notice that this strong wind sailing, exciting as it may be, places an unholy strain on the upper body. Even with a good stance with the arms straight, you probably lasted fifteen minutes before you had to come back in to shake some blood into the forearms. Fear not, strong wind windsurfing is not solely for body builders. The moment you are sailing comfortably in these stronger winds, you are ready to slip into a harness.

The most common design of harness fits you like a nappy. It has legstraps, it conforms to the shape of your bottom and has a hook on the front attached to a spreader bar at about belly-button height. You have two lines attached in a loop to either side of the boom. Once you are sailing you engage the hook in the loop, lean back and can use your whole body to combat the force in the rig whilst the arms are just used for making fine adjustments.

Harnesses help you to improve by giving you more time on the water. The effect they have on your stance and technique can be quite dramatic. If the lines are set up correctly, using a harness automatically places you in the correct strong wind stance and because you are using your whole body to counteract the sail, you can hold a bigger sail and go a lot faster.

Setting up the harness lines

The most convenient harness lines to buy have velcro or clamp
fastening buckles at each end to allow for easy adjustment and to
protect the rubber boom covering.

Your stance should look the same whether you are hooked in or out.
The lines must be long enough, therefore, to allow you to sail with straight
arms and maintain a good distance between your upper body and
the rig. They must be positioned so that the rig feels balanced with
an equal amount of pressure on both arms.

The depth of the loop will depend, of course, on the height you set
the boom and the length of your arms. As a general rule if you set
the boom at just under shoulder height, the depth of the line should
be roughly the same as your forearm, from the tip of your elbow to the
end of a clenched fist.

The apex of the loop should correspond to the balance point of the
rig. If you've got it right, in a steady wind you can let go with one or both
hands without the rig twisting away. This means your centre of gravity
is pulling directly against the centre of effort of the sail.

*Setting up the harness lines. With
the lines loosely attached, hold the
rig up on the beach. Move the
hands closer and closer together
until you can support it with one
hand. That is the balance point
of the boom*

*Then move the ends of the line so
they are equidistant from the
balance point just inside shoulder
width apart*

You should just be able to fit your forearm, from the tip of your elbow to the end of a clenched fist, inside the loop

Hooking in and out

The first time you hook in, the feeling may be at the same time one of joy at the sudden relief of pressure on the arms and panic at finding yourself locked to the rig.

Let me first put your mind at rest by assuring you that using a harness is not dangerous. If you do get pulled over the top of the sail, just relax and keep your head clear of the boom. The line will drop out of the hook as soon as it goes slack. Thanks to the 'V' shaped hook, the rope can't get tangled but if by some weird twist of fate the rope did get knotted, you can shed the harness in a second by popping the quick release buckles.

Hooking in. To engage the line in the hook, pull the rig towards you, bend the knees and push the hips forward ➡ *Then drop away from the rig again by extending your arms and settle into a normal stance taking the weight of the rig on your body*

The higher hook of the simple waist harness on the right is easier for learning. With its leg straps and extra bottom support, the seat harness on the left is more comfortable, more efficient although slightly more restricting

If the line is correctly positioned, you should be able to take one hand off the boom

Used correctly, a harness allows you to hold down a bigger sail and go faster

You've already discovered how quickly things happen in a strong wind. In the harness where your freedom is somewhat restricted, your responses have to be even quicker. Ease yourself gently into this new sensation by first practising in a force 3 wind — enough to hang your weight against, but not overpowering. In that moderate breeze consider the following points:

— Never cheat by using a hand to place the line under the hook, you'd never get away with it in a strong wind!

— When hooking in, always keep your weight committed to windward, bend the knees and pull the rig towards you to swing the line under the hook. If you bring your weight inboard towards the rig, you will be pulled forward off balance as the tension hits the line.

— Relax the arms and let the body take the strain. Try dropping a hand off the boom and trim the sail by swinging the body in and out like a pendulum.

— If ever you feel uneasy, you can unhook simply by pulling the rig towards you. The line drops away the moment it goes slack.

— As you gain confidence, practise engaging the line **without** looking down.

Troubleshooting

Harness technique is such an important part of strong wind sailing that it's worth isolating a few of the problems and pointing out the corrective measures.

Take note of these symptoms:

If the lines are too near the front of the boom the back arm will feel overloaded. In strong wind the sail backwinds and you keep getting slammed windward.

If the lines are too far back on the boom the front hand feels overloaded, you get pulled off balance forward and you have a tendency to oversheet. When adjusting the lines out on the water, move both ends in the appropriate direction so they stay just inside shoulder width apart.

If the lines are too long you'll keep hooking out by mistake, your arms will get tired and your bottom will tend to drag in the water.

If the loop is too short you'll be unable to straighten your arms, you'll feel cramped and will have trouble reacting to gusts.

Good harness technique opens the door to all kinds of harmless posing

Trick of the day

The Pirouette

If you're in a warm climate and are desperate to fall off to cool down, then try a pirouette. The pirouette involves releasing the boom before spinning through 360 degrees and catching it again. It's the freestylers' favourite since it can be slotted into all sorts of tacks and gybes in light or strong winds, on long and short boards.

From a beam reach, sheet out and pull the rig across to windward to the balance point

I suggest you try it in a moderate breeze to start with. It's an excellent way to start a sailing session since it warms you up and gets you in the right frame of mind.

The trick is to sail on a beam reach and first practise just pulling the rig over to the balance point before letting it go altogether and seeing how many times you can clap your hands before catching it again. You have to be able to balance the rig like this in the pirouette or you'll find it flat in the water by the time you come round.

For the pirouette itself, it's easier to turn away from the sail. Move your head first and try to focus on an object. This helps you to stay orientated. Then concentrate on getting a hand back on the boom as quickly as possible.

Pivoting on the back foot, spin away from the rig, turning the head first

Reach out for the boom, bend the knees for stability and sail on to raucous cheers from the beach!

WHAT HAPPENS NEXT?

Today's goals: Choosing your equipment — Avenues to follow; aspects of racing — Techniques to aspire to — Ways to improve.

Equipment: what there is and what you need

The enthused windsurfer walks into a windsurfing shop intent on setting himself up for a season's practice and falls out of it empty handed an hour later baffled by jargon, blinded by science and totally overwhelmed by an apparently endless choice.

There is a staggering variety of equipment available. But with a little realistic consideration, the choice need not be that difficult

On the dark side, such incidents are not rare. There is a vast range of designs cloaked in a veil of hi-tech mumbo jumbo, which can appear baffling if you have just entered the sport. On the bright side, the standard of manufacturing and design of modern equipment is superb. There has never been a better time to learn and improve and if you take into account where you will be sailing, your size, ambition and, of course, your wealth, you can very easily narrow down the options and make the right choice.

Boards

Length Boards vary in size from approximately 3.75 m down to 2.45 m. The smaller they are the less stable and the more difficult they are to sail. Those less than roughly 2.75 m (depending on the bulk of the sailor) will not support the weight of the rig and sailor when stationary and cannot be uphauled in the conventional way. To get these 'sinkers' going, the sailor has to perform a **waterstart**, whereby he lies in the water with the sail over his head and lets the wind pull him onto the board. Like a waterski, the board rises to the surface and supports him as it gathers speed. Short boards require a minimum force 4 wind to get them going and I will be pinpointing their advantages and shortcomings later on.

Volume The volume of the board is at least as important as its length. A common mistake is to buy a board which simply isn't buoyant enough for the sailor. Volume is measured in litres which may make more sense if I reveal that a litre of volume supports roughly 1 kg of weight. If a person weighing 70 kg stood on a 70 litre board, it would just float but add to that the weight of the rig, and it would disappear. A simple formula to remember is that if you want your board to perform well and be stable in light winds, it must contain at least 130 litres of RESERVE volume. That 70 kg person will therefore be looking to a board in excess of 200 litres.

Referring back to Friday's Beaufort Scale, you'll remember that long boards become hard to control in winds much above force 6. At that stage, shorter boards with less volume come into their own but only under the feet of expert sailors.

Types of board

The course racer or race board 3.65 m–3.75 m; 220 ltrs–235 ltrs.
Designed to win in triangle course racing, the course racer has to perform on all points of sailing. The latest models are a delight to sail being both light and incredibly fast for their size. Thanks to their volume, they go well in non-planing conditions and can support a big rig. The catch is that they tend to be at the top of the price range.

A choice of boards with a daggerboard. From left to right, a mid-length 3.30 m, 3.5 m allround funboard, a 3.70 m course racer and on the end a stable flat board excellent for learning

Allround funboard 3.40 m–3.65 m; 190 ltrs–220 ltrs. This is a detuned version of the above. Usually made from a less exotic, more robust, cheaper material it is an excellent option for the person who wants an inexpensive introduction to the sport. However, with all the essential trimmings such as retracting dagger, sliding mast-track and footstraps, it still takes a long time to grow out of the allround funboard.

Mid-length funboard 3.20 m–3.35 m; 140 ltrs–180 ltrs falls between two stools, being neither a long nor a short board. It is primarily aimed at the improving sailor who is only interested in winds of force 4 and above, who demands the extra speed and manoeuvrability of a shorter board yet still wants to uphaul it and sail it back home comfortably should the wind drop. Being a scaled down version of the course racer, it is also an excellent first time board for children and light adults.

The Lechner 3.90 m is the board all competitors use in the Olympic games. Named after its designer, the Lechner has a displacement hull with a rounded underwater shape similar to a dinghy. This high volume design (70 litres more than most race boards) delivers an incredible light wind performance especially to windward. It is, however, very unstable downwind on a choppy sea.

Penny Way, many times ladies champion, training on the voluminous Olympic Lechner board

Short boards

We class a short board as one under 3.0 m without a daggerboard. Although the larger ones can be uphauled, they are very unstable at rest. Given that they are all designed for winds above force 4, potential users should be confident strong wind sailors and be able to waterstart.

We categorise short boards by design characteristics rather than length and volume. Next to the various groups, I have quoted a common length and volume, but these can easily be scaled up or down to suit the size and volume of the sailor.

A parade of short boards. From left to right, a 295 cm production wave slalom, a 275 cm custom made slalom, a 280 cm production copy of a World Cup slalom board, a 265 cm production wave slalom, and on the end a no compromise 260 cm custom wave board

Slalom boards 2.80 m; 100 ltrs. Slalom involves racing across the wind and gybing around a figure of eight course. The boards, therefore, have to have good acceleration, a high top speed and smooth gybing characteristics — qualities which delight recreational sailors as well as competitors. Their speed makes them the preferred design for mushy waves. Not surprisingly the slalom board is the most popular short board design in the UK.

Wave boards 2.65 m; 80 ltrs. In waves, manoeuvrability is the all important trait. The wave itself provides the forward momentum and acceleration. Wave boards have a lot of 'rocker' or scoop in both the nose and tail. Nose rocker allows the board to ride smoothly over and down the waves, whilst tail rocker allows the board to pivot and make slashing, tight radius turns on the face of a wave. It is this rocker which also slows the board down. Wave boards are very specialised and only come into their own on big waves. On flat water and chop and small mushy waves they can be frustratingly slow to plane.

Wave slalom boards 2.70 m; 90 ltrs. As the name suggests, these are a compromise between the above two categories. They display a reasonable turn of speed and good acceleration but having slightly more rocker than the slalom board, they are more manoeuvrable. An excellent allround design for flat water and waves.

Speed boards are designed simply to go very fast, in very strong winds on flat water. Acceleration and manoeuvrability are unimportant compared to their ability to track straight and hold in the water at speeds up to 40 knots. Their most noticeable feature is their width, or lack of it. The smallest are just 11 inches wide, the same as a waterski. As a result, they require a high level of skill and fitness on the part of the sailor and need a strong, constant wind to get going.

Materials

Polyethylene in its crudest form is the material washing up bowls are made from. Used predominantly in mass produced recreational boards it is both cheap and durable. Although once considered too heavy to be used in the racing models, the process has been so refined that some polyethylene short boards are now turning in an extraordinary performance.

Hybrids Manufacturers in the past wrestled with the dilemma that materials such as epoxy and carbon which make boards light and stiff are also fragile with little impact resistance. Experimentation over the years has since led to the development of hybrid materials which

Boards are very strong but not indestructible! Here a custom board splits in two after a heavy jump to reveal the foam core, the fibreglass laminate and the wooden 'stringers' cut into the foam to add strength and stiffness — not quite enough in this case

manage to combine high performance with durability. In general these hybrids contain epoxy resin and fibreglass underneath a strong ASA or ABS plastic skin. Some builders will offer you two versions of the same board, the more expensive model containing a greater percentage of carbon.

Custom boards Custom boards are hand shaped from a block of foam and spray painted with motifs as diverse as your imagination. They are then laminated traditionally with fibreglass and polyester or epoxy resin. Most custom manufacturers cater for the short board market and offer a line of tried and tested standard shapes. However, if you so desire, you can have a board made to your own design or at least ask the shaper to interpret your ideas.

Sails

If the board is the chassis then the sail is the motor. They are both equally important for a good performance. Like boards, different sail designs excel in certain areas. Some are powerful and fast, others are highly manoeuvrable, others are a bit of both. Here are the main types.

Soft sails 'Soft' and 'hard' in the context of sails refer to the extent to which the sail is supported by battens. In 'hard' sails all the battens run from the leech right up to the mast. In a 'soft' sail there are just one or two leech battens in the main body of the sail leaving the front section by the mast unsupported. The advantages of such a design are that it's light (less battens), it's easy to throw around in tricky manoeuvres and that it can 'luff' or flap. This not only gives the novice visible signs of what the sail is doing, but it also gives the expert more instant power control. The sail spills wind more easily and is more sensitive to small trimming movements with the back hand.

A soft sail with unsupported luff. This model has the facility to take short or full length battens

The RAF. The tapered battens slide right past the mast to form a smooth foil shape on the leeward side of the sail. When the sail is tacked, the luff sleeve rotates and the battens assume the same profile on the other side

Fully battened RAF (Rotating Asymmetrical Foil) is the most popular recreational design being fast, stable and manoeuvrable. The principle of the sail is that, thanks to full length tapered battens and a rotating luff sleeve, the sail forms an excellent foil shape and therefore generates more power per square metre than a conventional design. The RAF is more stable and powerful than the soft sail although marginally less forgiving. With the shape fixed by the battens, it is hard to spill wind and there is a sudden surge of power as the battens flick around in tacks and gybes.

Camber induced sails are no-compromise speed and racing designs. The sail's leading edge, the one the wind hits first, is critical, being the area where most of the lift is generated. In an effort to make that entry curve as smooth as possible and to make the sail hold its shape even in the strongest gusts, one sailmaker came up with a system whereby pieces of plastic fitted inside and supported a wide luff tube. They are held onto the mast by batten tension and bend that luff area into a cleaner wing shape than the simpler RAF. In racing there's nothing to touch camber induced sails. However, their weight — the widened luff tube can fill up if left in the water — their positive feel and their lack of manoeuvrability do not make them a wise choice for the recreational sailor in search of an easy ride.

Roof-racking

The gear selected, you will need to transport it safely on the roof of your car. Buy a sturdy two-bar ladder rack and unless you have a board bag, fit some foam pads around the bars. Lift the board on upside down (fin facing up), nose facing forward. Lay the boom on top and the mast either on the top or beside the board. Then using webbing straps with

Buy a strong two-bar roof rack and tie the board, mast and boom on using thick webbing straps with camlock buckles

camlock buckles, lash it down. Above all do NOT use bungy ropes. At speed they can easily stretch and break. For security it's worth attaching a line from the towing eye at the front of the board to the bumper.

The Law You can be prosecuted for carrying an unstable load — eight boards on a Mini may well land you in court. Check how far your mast sticks out. If it projects further beyond either bumper than 1.07 m (3' 6'') you must attach a marker board.

Insurance All windsurfing shops can sell you insurance. A marine policy will cover your board against breakage and theft and most importantly it will cover the sailor against third-party claims up to a half a million pounds. It's worth noting that you get free third-party cover if you join the Royal Yachting Association.

Avenues to explore

Short board sailing

Once solely the domain of Hawaiian demi-gods, short board sailing is now within the reach of all sailors who are sailing at ease in the footstraps and using a harness in winds of force 4 and above.

The shock involved in hopping straight from a long board to a wave board could put you off the idea altogether, so ease yourself down gradually. A mid-length funboard (approximately 3.30 m) makes an excellent waterstart-learning platform. It's easy to manoeuvre in the water and if you fail in your attempts, you can always uphaul and sail home. Furthermore, the reduction in volume sharpens up your responses and forces you to trim the board and rig more precisely.

For your own safety, plan your short board initiation with care. Bereft of your daggerboard and having so little beneath your feet, you take on an extra physical and mental burden. The board naturally doesn't travel upwind as well, so given that you will take the odd plunge, you may have trouble getting back to your start point.

On a short board the tempo quickens. The board is so sensitive that you always have to be on your mettle, concentrating and totally committed. Stop to scratch your nose and it will sink; flex a buttock and it will start to turn. Such a pace puts a severe strain on your energy reserves and, as with most other activities, performance deteriorates with fatigue. Ponder the following precautions.

Venue Short boards may excel in waves, but for learning, flat water on which the board can accelerate faster, reach a higher top speed and remain directionally stable is vastly preferable. The act of sailing a short board in strong winds is *less* tiring than a long board. What exhausts the sailor is the falling and attempted waterstarts. Wherever possible, select a shallow venue where you are always in your depth.
In some shallow harbours and beaches at low tide, you will not only feel safer and more confident but, being able to beachstart away after every mishap, you'll save energy and enjoy a much longer and more fruitful sailing session.

Take heed of the fact that it's very difficult to self-rescue a short board. There's just not enough room to stow the rig. Breakages and other mishaps are easily overcome if you stick to Friday's safety code and if you adhere to one rule in particular: **Stay within 200 metres of the shore line**. All the fun is in the turning and manoeuvring, so there's rarely a need to venture further out than this.

Conditions Unstable gusty winds are an even worse enemy than waves. You never get a chance to settle into the straps and in the lulls, the board will sink and head up into wind. Choose a venue open to the prevailing wind and try to select a launch site which allows you to launch across the wind. Due to the short board's poor windward performance, be especially wary of offshore winds.

Ideal short board conditions consist of a constant wind of force 5 or more. Once planing, they are actually easier to control in heavy seas than long boards

Funboard manoeuvres

Over the past week, you have reached the stage where you are starting to handle the board with some authority in planing winds. Now the sport really comes alive, as a whole syllabus of dynamic manoeuvres awaits you, some essential, others unashamedly flamboyant. Here are a few to whet your appetite.

The waterstart as well as being the only way to get a short board going, is also the best way to get any board going in strong winds. When you uphaul you are always pulling against the wind which is trying to blow the rig back down into the water. With the rig out of the water you then have to struggle to maintain balance on a choppy sea as you move into the sailing position. In the waterstart you go with the flow, and let the wind do the work. Furthermore, you rise up straight into your sailing position with power in the sail. It's best when learning to split the skill into two sections: freeing the rig from the water and the start itself. The first part relies on you swimming the rig into a position where the mast is at right angles to the wind. You then draw it up and into wind to allow wind to blow right under the sail.

The start itself is like a deep water beachstart. You manoeuvre the board just off the wind using mastfoot pressure before placing your back foot on. You then throw the rig up and forwards to expose

The waterstart is the quickest way of getting all boards going in strong winds

the whole area to the wind, rock up over your bent back leg and rise up under the boom. With practice you can have fallen and be sailing again within five seconds.

The carve gybe is windsurfing's premier manoeuvre. The basic technique is the same for long and short boards although it is the one skill that world champions and funboard novices alike continually struggle to perfect. It is a downwind turn where the sailor, at full planing speed, banks the board into the turn by digging in the leeward (inside) edge with his back foot. When the board has carved through the wind and is heading on the new broad reach, the sailor changes his feet and flips the rig around. If his balance, timing and commitment are spot on, he will exit still on the plane. It is a superb feeling similar to turning a surfboard, a snow ski or even a motorbike. It is a watershed in technique terms in that this is the first manoeuvre in the book where the sailor has nothing to lean against. He has to commit himself and the rig right to the inside of the turn and rely on the centrifugal force to keep him upright. To master it you just have to get your hair wet and obey the windsurfer's favourite maxim, Go For It!

The carve gybe is the very essence of funboard sailing. Banking the board and rig over, you throw up a plume of spray and, mishaps aside, you swoop through the turn like a waterskier

The duck gybe is a flashy variation of the carve gybe where you duck under the foot of the sail as the board carves downwind rather than letting it swing over the front. It's best suited to short boards.

In the duck gybe you pass under the foot of the sail rather than letting it swing around the front

The carving 360 is a totally useless but thoroughly enjoyable short board stunt where board, rig and sailor keep carving right through 360 degrees to end up facing the direction from where they started. The entry is the same as the carve gybe, only instead of flicking the rig around, the sailor lays it down to leeward so the wind fills from the other side. He stays in that position pushing against the sail before falling back against the rig as it turns through the last 90 degrees — ten out of ten for posing!

Half way through the carving 360 the sailor ends up front to sail and is about to steer through the last 180 degrees using the rig — a lot of fun and fuss to end up going in the original direction

The slam gybe by contrast is a very useful turn where the sailor slows right down, places the back foot right back on the tail, leans back and, sheeting in hard 'slams' the tail into the water. In a plume of spray the board spins around and the sailor moves forward quickly to kill the rotation before flipping the rig. It is simply a dynamic version of the long board flare gybe and is the quickest way to turn the board round on the spot.

The aerial gybe as the name suggests is a mid-air gybe. The sailor heads into wind before taking off from a wave or a piece of chop. At the apex of the jump he twists the board in the air with his feet and lands with the sail clew first heading in the new direction. No better way has yet been discovered to stretch ankle ligaments.

In the aerial gybe the board is turned in mid air and ankles are tweaked on landing

Wave sailing

At the top end of windsurfing's acrobatic scale lies wave sailing, a mixture of sailing, surfing and hang-gliding. It is essentially the domain of the manoeuvrable short board. Long boards are not natural fliers and are simply too unwieldy in breaking surf where the turns often need to be short and sharp.

Getting airborne The first skill to learn is jumping. It is not difficult to leave the water; indeed such is the inevitable result of a board hitting a ramp at 25 mph. What is more difficult is the in-flight control and the landing. On take-off, the sailor bends his legs, drops his weight and stays sheeted in. He then controls the trajectory with his feet, dragging the tail up under his bottom to bear the board away and land just off the wind. To protect board and knees, it's best to extend the back foot slightly on landing to touch down tail first. The back then sinks and absorbs the shock.

You can make massive jumps off the smallest waves if you let the wind blow under the board and sail the board through the air

115

With the basic jump under your belt, you can only be limited by your imagination and your desire for self preservation. The 'in' manoeuvre is currently the 'aerial loop'. Once considered impossible, now wave sailors the world over are blasting off wave tops and completing full somersaults, forwards and backwards with their boards and rigs. A few have even successfully landed a double loop.

Forward and backward loops where board, rig and rider perform a complete mid air somersault were considered impossible as little as five years ago. Now people are going for doubles!

Wave riding is windsurfing returning to its surfing roots. Having leaped and somersaulted his way out through the waves, the sailor then turns around and picks up an unbroken wave. His aim, thereafter, is to ride the face performing a series of short and long radius turns at the top and bottom of the wave, staying as close to white water as possible.

The wild west coasts of England, Wales, Scotland and Ireland are popular venues. The mecca, however, is Hawaii and the island of Maui where mountainous waves pound onto the coral reefs.

The waverider performs the same moves on the wave face as the pure surfer. His aim is to make long and tight radius turns as near to the steepest section of the wave as possible

Racing

As a competitive sport windsurfing is incredibly mature for its tender years. In 1984, just 15 years old, windsurfing became the youngest sport ever to be granted Olympic status. In Los Angeles, the boards competed around the same courses, to the same rules, as the other yachting classes. Windsurfing is also a highly developed professional sport. Every year the world's top sailors compete on a World Tour similar to golf and tennis, for prize money in excess of two million dollars. It's big business with results being linked closely to the sales of certain brands of equipment. In the UK, racing takes place at club, regional, national and professional level. Even if you have avoided competitive situations like the plague all of your life, it is really worth giving it a go at club level. Not only is it great fun, but it's undoubtedly the best way to improve and sharpen up your technique.

Like athletics, windsurfing has many different competitive disciplines. Here is a brief description of the options open to you.

Triangle racing is the most common racing format taking place on coastal and inland venues, predominantly on long boards. Everyone starts together and heads upwind to the windward mark, before sailing down two or four downwind legs, depending on the course. For this type of racing there is a book of rules. Fear not, you only need to know two or three simple ones to get started. The skill lies first in making your board go fast and then in trying to secure a tactical advantage over your competitors. As you improve, you learn to read the windshifts and make use of the tidal flow. With as many as a hundred other competitors on the course, your steering and manoeuvring skills are tested to the limit.

In light or strong winds, there is no better way to improve your board handling, your speed and your wind awareness than course racing

117

Slalom is run on short boards across the wind usually around a figure of eight course on flat water or in breaking surf. It is a knock-out contest. Heats of eight sailors complete two or three laps of the course with the top four getting through to the next round. Slalom is becoming increasingly popular due to the speed and excitement of the racing, the spectator appeal and the ease of organisation. Although less tactically demanding than triangle racing, from the sailor's point of view slalom is the ultimate test of board handling and gybing.

A running 'Le Mans' style start to a slalom race. Figure of eight slalom on flat water or in breaking surf is popularly considered the most exciting racing discipline

Freestyle is a fun way to improve your funboard skills in light winds. In competition, tricks like this backwards railride have to be strung together to form a flowing routine

Wave performance, like gymnastics or ice skating, takes place before a panel of trained judges. In heats lasting about ten minutes, two or four competitors go out into the surf to display their expertise. They are marked in three areas — jumping, wave riding and transitions (how they turn round). Although it appears like a tailor-made playground for lunatics, wave competition is very tactical. You have to complete a certain number of jumps and rides in a limited time. You have to time your runs so you pick the best waves and you have to stay cool under the pressure of competition. Many sailors waste time going for outrageous stunts and spend most of the heat swimming instead of sailing within their ability and performing tricks they are confident of completing.

Freestyle was pushed into the background by the arrival of short boards but has made something of a comeback as a perfect light wind alternative to slalom and wave sailing. At the end of each day we have been attempting simple tricks. In a competition you have to fit such tricks into a three minute routine, during which time the judges will mark you on difficulty of tricks, style, fluidity, originality and entertainment value.

Former world record holder Eric Beale shoots down the famous Sotavento speed course in the Canaries on a board just 13 inches wide. For the last four years a board has held the overall speed record for wind powered craft

Speed sailing is perhaps the purest of all the disciplines being a simple test of straight line speed. In competition, you sail flat out between transits usually 500 m or 250 m apart and your average time is calculated. During the day you can have as many attempts as you can fit in. Speed sailing is very popular because you do not have to be an acrobatic wizard to compete at a high level. In the top echelons, however, it has become very specialised. In 1986 a board became the fastest wind-powered watercraft when Frenchman Pascal Maka broke the 36 knot world record held by the catamaran *Crossbow*. He has since pushed that record up to an astonishing 42 knots (nearly 50 mph). Speed competitions can be held on any open water on any boards, but world records demand the highest tech boards and rigs and immaculate conditions in the form of a force 8 gale (40 knots of wind) blowing at an angle of 120–130 degrees to perfectly flat water. The French were so keen to snatch the record that they built a canal in the south of France at a perfect angle to the *mistral* wind.

Ways to improve

There is so much to try in windsurfing yet many people throw in the towel after a few years, fed up with making the same old mistakes, convinced in their own minds that they'll never get any better. Such an attitude tends to be a self-fulfilling prophecy as they then settle onto a plateau and stop trying. Yes, tackling mast-high waves and landing loops does take a certain amount of God-given athleticism, but what many consider to be impossibly advanced manoeuvres can be achieved by structuring your sessions, by looking at your performance more analytically and by periodically seeking some outside help.

Consolidate the basics Continual problems with advanced techniques such as the carve gybe can invariably be traced back to a poor basic stance. There is a compelling temptation in windsurfing to run before you can walk. People hop on short boards and frequently attempt advanced manoeuvres before their basic board and rig control are sound.

Speed at all costs Windsurfing differs from many other activities in that life becomes easier the faster you go. When you are sailing slowly relative to the windspeed, not only is there considerable force in the rig, but there will be a lot of board in contact with water making it very reluctant to footsteer and carve gybe.

There is no better way to improve your speed than sparring with a friend. When someone tries to overtake you, you immediately start to try harder, sheet in a little more, trim the board flatter and concentrate on the waves and on giving the board as smooth a ride as possible.

Bringing on the expert Some people who are reluctant to seek outside help sentence themselves to a life in a rut. Most of us are not particularly good at teaching ourselves. We may read about the technique and watch an expert in action, but the problem is that we often have a very false image of ourselves in action. **What we feel like is often** NOT **what we look like**.

When you do hit that learning plateau, you are well advised to go back to school and attend an RYA level 2, 3, 4 or 5 course. At the funboard levels for example, manoeuvres such as the waterstart and carve gybe are broken down on a funboard simulator. You are then sent out to practise certain elements at a time. The best teaching aid of all is the video playback facility. Your attempts are filmed, after which the instructor analyses your performance. Before you stands the irrefutable evidence in glorious Technicolor of that wayward front hand or the straight legs. Incredulous, shocked yet enlightened, you are immediately inspired to do something about it.

Make the most of what you've got It's a problem that befalls many sailors that having experienced the exhilaration of sailing short boards in high winds, they can think of nothing else and devote their leisure time solely to that end. That's fine if you live in Hawaii, but in Europe you may spend many weeks waiting for your day off to coincide with a wind, during which time you get frustrated, bored and ultimately disenchanted. The lesson that many have learned is to hang onto their long boards and get out on the water no matter what the windstrength. So many of the trendy short board manoeuvres have their roots in freestyle. The duck gybe, duck tack, helicopter tack to name a few, can all be practised and learned on a long board in light winds. On a long board you can go racing or cruising in a group. It's social, enjoyable and all the time you're improving your skills.